INDIANAPOLIS
COLLECTS & COOKS

The Alliance of The Indianapolis Museum of Art.

Cover:
Sumba Island, Indonesia
Hinggi (Men's Wrapper) late 19th
    or early 20th Century
cotton ikat dyed warp faced plain weave
Sarah L. and Eliza M. Niblack Collection
Indianapolis Museum of Art, 33.628

The groups and societies offering the suggested menus are all
supportive of the Museum and sponsor Museum events, lectures,
study programs and undertake projects to acquire purchase
funds for new acquisitions. Membership in these volunteer
groups is open to all members of The Indianapolis Museum of Art.

Copyright © 1980 by Alliance Publications,
The Alliance of the Indianapolis Museum of Art,
Indianapolis, Indiana
Library of Congress Catalog Card Number: 80-65179
(ISBN: 0-936260-00-9)
Editor: Cookbook Committee, 1979
Designed by Joseph Smith
Photography by Robert Wallace
Typography by Weimer Typesetting Co., Inc., Indianapolis
The type fonts used are the Garamond and Helvetica series.
Second printing 1983 by Design Printing Co., Inc.

Art finds expression in an infinite variety of ways, and what a treat is in store for you in this book. The representative sampling from the Museum's collections tempts the eye, but the splendid display of culinary art which these recipes denote, tempts the palate with the promise of the art of creative dining. This book is the culmination of a two and a half year project undertaken with love and with the famous gusto and verve that mark every activity of the Museum's incomparable Alliance. Three hundred and twenty members of the IMA submitted more than 1100 recipes for the book, and from them 301 of the very best were selected for this publication and are presented here for your pleasure. Our thanks to all those who helped in this project and our gratitude and admiration to those who brought it to such a successful completion are without measure. To all of you who will benefit from the fruits of this labor of love—Enjoy! Enjoy!

Robert A. Yassin
Director
Indianapolis Museum of Art

Robert Indiana, American, 1928-
LOVE, 1970
cor-ten steel, 144 x 144 x 72 inches
Gift of friends of the Indianapolis Museum of Art in memory of Henry F. DeBoest 75.174

CONTENTS
Appetizers 1
Soups and Sandwiches 27
Brunch, Lunch, and Supper 57
Entrées and Accompaniments 69
Sauces 103
Vegetables 105
Salads and Salad Dressings 133
Breads 147
Desserts 167
Relishes, Pickles, and Jellies 195

APPETIZERS

MUSHROOM-FILLED PASTRY (Piroshki)

Yield: 36

Pastry
1 cup butter
8 ounces cream cheese
¼ cup heavy cream
2½ cups flour
½ teaspoon salt

Mushroom Filling
½ cup finely chopped onions
3 tablespoons butter
½ lb. mushrooms, chopped
2 tablespoons flour
¼ teaspoon thyme
½ teaspoon salt
¼ teaspoon pepper
¼ cup cream

Seal
1 egg
¼ cup milk

Cream together butter and cream cheese. Beat in heavy cream. Add flour and salt. Blend thoroughly. Roll into ball, cover, and chill several hours or overnight. Roll dough in small amounts between wax paper sheets. Cut with cookie or biscuit cutter and fill each pastry. Fold in half-moon shape, then seal with egg-milk mixture. Brush rest of egg-milk on top of sealed pastries. Bake at 400°F on ungreased cookie sheets for 12 to 20 minutes.

Mushroom Filling: Sauté onions until transparent in butter. Add mushrooms. Cook mixture 3 minutes. Stir in flour, thyme, salt, and pepper. Add cream and let thicken. Remove immediately from heat. Serve hot. May be frozen.

FRIED CAMEMBERT HORS D'OEUVRES

Serves 6

6 ounces Camembert cheese, chilled
2 eggs, lightly beaten
¾ cup dry bread crumbs
Vegetable oil

Cut cold cheese into twelve wedges. Dip each wedge in beaten egg, then into bread crumbs. Repeat. Heat oil to 375°F in deep saucepan or deep fat fryer. Fry cheese wedges about 1 minute or until crispy brown. Drain on paper towels. Serve warm.

Quick, easy, and delicious. May be served with hot mustard sauce or a sweet and sour sauce.

BAKED MUSHROOMS WITH BLEU CHEESE

Serves 4 to 6

1 lb. mushrooms, about 1-inch
  diameter
½ lb. bleu cheese
5 to 6 slices bacon, fried crisp

Clean mushrooms with a damp towel. Cut off end of stem if tough. Place in 1-quart casserole, and top with crumbled cheese and bacon pieces. Heat at 450°F for 15 minutes.

Serve with toothpicks as hors d'oeuvre or as a meat accompaniment.

HOT MUSHROOM DIP

Serves 8

1 lb. mushrooms
6 tablespoons butter
1 medium onion, minced
  Salt
  Pepper
3 tablespoons flour
1 cup sour cream
½ teaspoon Worcestershire sauce

Wash and slice mushrooms. Sauté in butter with onions over low flame. Season with salt and pepper, and sprinkle flour over mushroom mixture. Stir gently and cook 3 minutes. Add sour cream and Worcestershire sauce. Heat until mixture thickens; this is a short time.

Serve in a chafing dish surrounded by crackers. This can be made a day or two before a party and reheated over low heat.

CREAM CHEESE WITH CHUTNEY DIP

Yield: 1¼ Cups

3 ounces cream cheese
  softened
½ pint sour cream
3 tablespoons chutney
1 teaspoon curry powder
  Dash of chili powder
  Squeeze of lemon

Mix all ingredients well and chill.

Serve with fresh vegetables or your favorite crackers.

BROILED MUSHROOM CANAPÉS

Serves 12 to 15

1 lb. mushrooms or 4 cans: 4
    oz. each
8 tablespoons butter
8 ounces cream cheese
2 egg yolks
½ teaspoon minced garlic
½ teaspoon salt
    Bread rounds or sliced bread,
      cut in quarters

Finely chop mushrooms and brown in butter. Drain, save butter. Mix cream cheese, egg yolks, garlic, and salt into a paste; and set aside. Butter bread rounds or quarters with butter drained from mushrooms. Toast, buttered side up, under broiler. Watch carefully! Remove from oven, add mushrooms to paste, and put on untoasted side of bread. Toast again.

MUSHROOMS À LA GRECQUE

Serves 6

1½ lbs. whole small mushrooms
½ teaspoon rosemary
2 cups water
½ teaspoon sage
1 cup olive oil
1 branch fennel
2 tablespoons lemon juice
1 tablespoon white vinegar
1 stalk celery
1 clove garlic, peeled
½ teaspoon thyme
½ bay leaf
¾ teaspoon freshly ground
    coriander
8 peppercorns
¾ teaspoon salt

Combine all ingredients and bring to a boil. Simmer, stirring occasionally, 5 minutes. Pour into a bowl, and marinate overnight in the refrigerator.
    Serve the mushrooms on toothpicks or as a first course on a bed of lettuce leaves.

INDIANAPOLIS COLLECTS & COOKS

MARINATED MUSHROOMS

Yield: 2 Cups

⅓ cup red wine vinegar
⅓ cup salad oil
1 small onion, sliced thin and
  separated
1 teaspoon salt
2 teaspoons dried parsley flakes
1 teaspoon prepared mustard
1 tablespoon brown sugar
2 cans mushroom tops, drained
  (the larger the better): 6 oz.
  each

Combine all ingredients except mushrooms in a saucepan, and bring to boil. Add mushrooms and simmer 5 to 6 minutes. Chill in covered bowl for several hours. Stir occasionally. Drain.

Serve on toothpicks as appetizer. Can be used in salads. May be served immediately if in a hurry.

CHEESE PUFFS

Yield: 50 1-inch Cubes

1 loaf white bread, unsliced
½ cup butter, softened
3 ounces cream cheese,
  softened
½ cup grated sharp cheddar
  cheese
¼ teaspoon dry mustard
¼ teaspoon cayenne
  Salt
2 egg whites, stiffly beaten

Trim crust from bread, and cut loaf into 1-inch cubes. In heavy saucepan combine butter, cheeses, and seasonings. Heat mixture over low heat, stirring until cheese is just melted and ingredients are well blended. Transfer mixture to bowl, and fold in egg whites. Dip bread cubes into mixture, coating well. Place on buttered baking sheets. Chill overnight covered loosely with foil. Freeze at this point in sealed plastic bags, if desired. Bake in preheated oven 400°F for 8 to 10 minutes or until golden brown.

Appetizers

CHEESE TRIANGLES (Tiropitta)

Yield: 60

15 ounces feta cheese
1 lb. farmer, dry cottage, or
  ricotta cheese
1 onion, grated: 2 to 3
  tablespoons
1 tablespoon minced parsley
1 large egg or 2 small
1 lb. package phyllo pastry,
  defrosted
1 cup melted butter
1 egg, beaten

Rinse feta cheese and crumble. Cream together cheeses, onion, and parsley. Add egg (or eggs). Beat until smooth. (This can be done in a food processor using the steel blade.) Refrigerate cheese mixture several hours or overnight to firm it. When ready to make triangles lay phyllo flat on a slightly damp dish towel and keep covered at all times; otherwise, the pastry will dry and crumble. Cut each sheet horizontally into 3 strips and brush each with melted butter. Place a heaped teaspoon of the cheese mixture on the lower corner of one strip. Fold over one corner to make a triangle. Continue folding pastry strip from side to side in the shape of a triangle until entire pastry strip covers the filling. (Make sure top of strip is well buttered to make pastry stick.) Proceed in this manner with phyllo strips and filling until all are used. (You might have some pastry or filling left over depending on the condition of the dough.) Place triangles seam down on unbuttered cookie sheet, and brush with beaten egg. Bake at 350°F for about 15 minutes or a little longer, until brown if you are going to serve them immediately. If you are going to freeze them, bake only until blond, so they can brown when reheated.

Serve hot and provide plenty of paper napkins. They freeze beautifully. No need to defrost. Bake them frozen.

CHEESE MOUSSE

Yield: 3 Cups

1 envelope gelatin
1½ cups beef broth
1 clove garlic, sliced
¼ teaspoon curry powder
⅛ teaspoon white pepper
12 ounces cream cheese

Sprinkle gelatin on cool broth in a pan, and let stand a few minutes to soften. Bring almost to a boil, stirring to dissolve gelatin completely. Cool. Put broth, garlic, curry powder, and pepper in blender. Blend ½ minute. Add cream cheese one-third at a time while blender is running. When blended, give final burst of speed. Pour into a 3-cup mold or loaf pan. Refrigerate 3 hours or until mousse is set. Unmold on lettuce. Decorate with black olive slices, and serve with toast or crackers.

CHESTER CAKES

Yield: 30 to 36

1 cup butter, softened
½ lb. sharp cheddar cheese, grated
2 cups sifted all-purpose or unbleached flour
Few dashes cayenne
Filling
1½ cups grated sharp cheddar cheese
½ cup butter, softened
1 tablespoon dry sherry
Dash of cayenne
Salt

Combine all ingredients. Mix well. Wrap dough in foil, and chill 1 hour. Roll out to ¼-inch thickness on lightly floured board or pastry marble. Cut into 1½-inch rounds. Bake rounds on foil-covered cookie sheet at 350°F for 15 to 20 minutes or until they are golden. Let the rounds cool on a wire rack.
Filling: In a bowl combine filling ingredients until mixture is creamy. Spread a little of filling on half of the rounds. Top with the remaining rounds. Store in airtight container in refrigerator. Bring to room temperature before serving.
Great with soup.

Appetizers

HUNGARIAN CHEESE

Yield: 2 Cups

8 ounces cream cheese
4 tablespoons butter
½ cup large curd cottage cheese
1 teaspoon prepared mustard
1 green onion, finely minced
1½ teaspoons caraway seed
1½ teaspoons paprika
    Salt

Soften cheese and butter, then mix in other ingredients.
    This may be served as an appetizer with crisp vegetable strips, as a sandwich spread, or as a salad on fresh greens.

SPICED COCKTAIL CHEESE

Serves 8 to 10

8 ounces cream cheese at
    room temperature
2 ounces Roquefort or bleu
    cheese
1 scant tablespoon sweet
    paprika (Hungarian)
1 tablespoon grated red onion
1 teaspoon Dijon mustard
3 to 4 tablespoons sour cream
2 teaspoons caraway seeds
    (optional)
3 tablespoons chopped chives

Combine all ingredients except chives, and mix until well blended. Refrigerate.
    If the cheese is to be used as a spread, shape it into a mound and decorate it with the chopped chives; or shape it into a ball and roll in the chives.

WATER CHESTNUT SPREAD

Yield: 3 Cups

1 cup sour cream
1 cup mayonnaise
1 can water chestnuts,
    diced: 8 oz.
1 bunch green onions, chopped
1 tablespoon soy sauce
1 teaspoon Worcestershire sauce
    Dash of Tabasco

Mix all ingredients. Serve with crackers.
    Fresh water chestnuts add a different taste to this dish.

INDIANAPOLIS COLLECTS & COOKS

TOMATO CHEESE SPREAD

Serves 10 to 12

2 tablespoons butter
1 can tomato paste: 6 oz.
¾ cup grated cheeses, such as
  Romano, Parmesan, etc.
¼ cup chopped parsley
¼ teaspoon salt
¼ teaspoon paprika
  Dash of cayenne pepper
  Additional parsley for garnish

Soften butter and combine with tomato paste. Add cheeses, chopped parsley, and seasonings. Refrigerate at least one hour. Keeps overnight. Place in a deep bowl, and decorate with chopped parsley.
Serve with rye crackers or bread.

CHUTNEY CURRY SPREAD

Serves 10 to 12

8 ounces cream cheese
4 ounces cheddar cheese,
  grated
4 tablespoons sherry
½ teaspoon curry powder
¼ teaspoon salt
2 green onions, minced
  Chutney

Soften cheese to room temperature. Mix all ingredients except chutney. Spread one-half-inch thick on serving plate. Cover with chutney.
Serve with crackers.

MARINATED ONIONS AND BLEU CHEESE

Serves 4 to 5

½ cup olive oil
2 tablespoons lemon juice
1 teaspoon salt
  Dash of pepper
  Dash of paprika
½ teaspoon sugar
¼ cup crumbled bleu cheese
2 cups thinly sliced large red onions

Mix oil, lemon juice, seasonings, and sugar. Stir in bleu cheese. Pour over onions, cover, and chill at least two days.
This is a nice side dish for a picnic. Serve with pumpernickel and unsalted butter.

Appetizers

CRAB OR SHRIMP MOLD

Yield: 4-Cup Mold

11 ounces cream cheese
3 tablespoons mayonnaise
1½ tablespoons lemon juice
1 envelope gelatin
3 tablespoons cold water
1 lb. cooked shrimp, chopped,
    or ½ lb. crab meat
½ cup chopped celery
1 small onion, chopped
1 green pepper, chopped
2 hard cooked eggs, chopped
  Salt
  Pepper
½ teaspoon Tabasco

Combine cream cheese, mayonnaise, lemon juice. Dissolve gelatin in cold water over hot water or low heat. Add remaining ingredients and season to taste. Pour into lightly oiled mold. Set in refrigerator until firm.

Serve with crackers.

CRAB MEAT QUICHE

Yield: 9-inch Pie

3 eggs, slightly beaten
1 cup sour cream
½ teaspoon Worcestershire
    sauce
¾ teaspoon salt
1 cup shredded Swiss cheese
1 can crab meat or frozen,
    thawed: 6½ oz.
1 can French fried onions: 3 oz.
1 9-inch pastry shell, baked

Combine eggs, sour cream, Worcestershire sauce, and salt. Stir in cheese, crab meat, and onions. Pour into pie shell. Bake at 300°F 55 to 60 minutes or until a silver knife inserted in center comes out clean.

This quiche reheats well in a microwave oven.

INDIANAPOLIS COLLECTS & COOKS

CURRY DIP FOR VEGETABLES

Yield: 1 Cup

1 cup mayonnaise
1 teaspoon tarragon vinegar
1 teaspoon horseradish
1 teaspoon grated onion
1 teaspoon grated garlic
1 tablespoon curry (or less for
    milder flavor)

Mix all ingredients thoroughly in a small bowl. Refrigerate at least 2 hours before serving.
    Serve with raw vegetables.

COTTAGE CHEESE BOURBON DIP

Yield: 1½ Cups

1 carton cottage cheese: 8 oz.
2 teaspoons bourbon whiskey
2 tablespoons light cream
2 tablespoons lemon juice
1 teaspoon grated onion
    Dash salt
2 dashes Tabasco
2 tablespoons chopped chives

Put small amount cottage cheese and all other ingredients except chives in blender. Blend and when mixture is smooth, add remaining cottage cheese a spoonful at a time with blender running. When mixture is smooth, stir in chives. Store in refrigerator, covered.
    May substitute sour cream or softened cream cheese for cottage cheese.

MIDGET HAMBURGERS

Yield: 40

10 slices of sandwich bread
4 tablespoons butter
1 lb. ground chuck
1 tablespoon Worcestershire
    sauce
1 teaspoon salt

Toast bread on one side only. Cut 4 rounds from each slice with a cookie cutter (1½ inch). Butter untoasted sides only slightly. Mix chuck, Worcestershire, and salt. Shape into 40 tiny balls. Place one on buttered side of each round. Broil 4 inches from heat for 5-6 minutes. Serve hot.
    Offer with a variety of toppings such as chutney, green onions, olives, chopped anchovies...use your imagination!

Appetizers

HOT ARTICHOKE DIP

Yield: 3 Cups

1 can artichoke hearts, drained:
   14 oz.
1 jar mayonnaise: 16 oz.
1 cup Parmesan cheese, grated
   Garlic salt (optional)

Mash artichokes with fork. Mix with mayonnaise, cheese, and garlic salt. Bake at 350°F for 15 minutes or until cheese is melted.
   Serve with crackers or party rye. So-o-o good . . . everyone wonders what is in it!

ARTICHOKE APPETIZER

Yield: 24

24 melba rounds, plain or garlic
1 can artichokes, drained:
   6½ oz.
¼ cup mayonnaise
1 tablespoon artichoke juice
   Parmesan cheese
   Paprika

Slice artichokes in ¼-inch slices. Place on rounds. Combine mayonnaise and artichoke juice. Cover the artichoke slices with the above mixture. Sprinkle lightly with Parmesan cheese and paprika. Place on cookie sheet, and put under preheated broiler.
   Watch closely—they brown quickly.

SPINACH DIP

Serves 8 to 10

1 package chopped frozen
   spinach: 10 oz.
1 cup sour cream
8 ounces cream cheese
¼ cup chopped parsley
½ teaspoon dill weed (or more
   to taste)
1 to 2 tablespoons lemon juice
1 package dried leek soup mix:
   2¾ oz.

Defrost and drain spinach. Mix with remaining ingredients.
   Serve on thin slices of toasted bagel with raw vegetables or crackers.

INDIANAPOLIS COLLECTS & COOKS

GALA MUSEUM OPENING

Champagne
Nova Scotia Salmon Mold
Hot Mushroom Dip
Spinach Dip
Raw Vegetables
Spiced Cocktail Cheese

PARMESAN CHEESE LEAVES

Yield: 24

1 cup flour
½ cup butter
1 cup grated Parmesan cheese
¼ teaspoon salt
2 tablespoons cold water
1 egg, slightly beaten

In medium bowl combine the flour and butter that has been cut into small pieces. With pastry blender or two knives cut butter into flour until butter particles are the size of small peas. With fork stir in cheese and salt. Sprinkle evenly with cold water. Toss with a fork. Form into a ball with hands, then flatten slightly. Between sheets of wax paper on a slightly damp surface, roll out to ¼-inch thickness. Using leaf-shape or small cookie cutters, cut out pastry. Place in plastic freezer container with wax paper between layers. Cover and freeze. When ready to use, preheat oven to 400°F. Place about 1 inch apart on ungreased cookie sheets. Brush tops with egg lightly. Bake, still frozen, 10 minutes or until golden. Serve warm.

Appetizers

SUTPHIN FOUNTAIN AT NIGHT
Stuart O. Dawson, Designer
dedicated 25 October 1972
Given by the Sutphin family in memory of Samuel Brady Sutphin

Francisco Jose de Goya y Lucientes, Spanish, 1746-1828
PORTRAIT OF DON FELIX COLON DE LARREATEGUI, 1794
oil on canvas, 43 5/8 x 33 1/8 inches
Gift of The Krannert Charitable Trust, 75.454

Paul Cézanne, French, 1839-1906
HOUSE IN PROVENCE, ca. 1885
oil on canvas, 25½ x 32 inches
Gift of Mrs. James W. Fesler in memory of Daniel W. and Elizabeth C. Marmon, 45.194

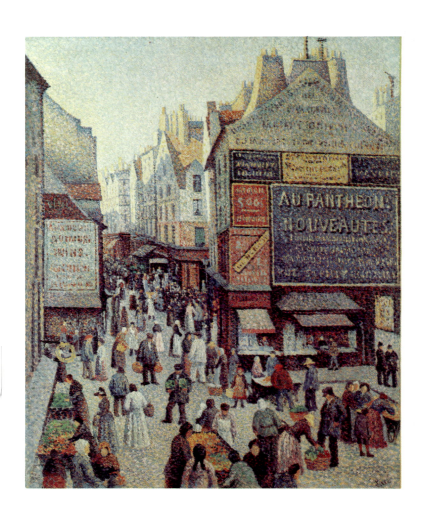

Maximilien Luce, French, 1858-1941
LA RUE MOUFFETARD, 1889-1890
oil on canvas
The Holliday Collection, 79.331

STUFFED CUCUMBERS (GURKAS NORGE)

Serves 6 to 8

2 small cucumbers
12 anchovies or 1 tube anchovy
  paste
1 tablespoon fresh dill
1 tablespoon fresh chives
6 ounces cream cheese
  Salt
  Freshly ground pepper
½ pint sour cream
  Red caviar

Slice cucumbers lengthwise. Seed and cut in bite-sized lengths. Mash anchovies and mix in dill, chives, and cream cheese softened with 2 tablespoons of the sour cream. Season with salt and pepper to taste. Fill cucumbers with this mixture, and top with sour cream and caviar.

Garnish with lemon wedges and parsley. Good with Bloody Marys.

SAVORY BEEF STUFFED CHERRY TOMATOES

Yield: 24

24 cherry tomatoes
3 ounces chipped beef
8 ounces cream cheese,
  softened
1 teaspoon Worcestershire
  sauce
1 tablespoon chopped chives
  Parsley, chopped

Core cherry tomatoes; remove pulp and seeds, and turn them upside down to drain. Chill. Finely chop beef and blend with cream cheese. Season with Worcestershire sauce and chives. Stuff tomatoes with cheese mixture, and sprinkle with parsley. Refrigerate until ready to serve.

INDIANAPOLIS COLLECTS & COOKS

SWEET AND SOUR COCKTAIL MEATBALLS

Yield: 4 Dozen

1 lb. lean ground beef
½ cup dry bread crumbs
½ cup minced onion
¼ cup milk
1 egg
1 tablespoon chopped parsley
1 teaspoon salt
⅛ teaspoon pepper
½ teaspoon Worcestershire
   sauce
¼ cup shortening
1 bottle chili sauce: 12 oz.
1 jar grape jelly: 10 oz.

Mix ground beef, bread crumbs, onion, milk, egg, parsley, salt, pepper, and Worcestershire sauce. Shape into one-inch balls. Melt shortening in large skillet. Brown meatballs. Remove meatballs from skillet; pour off fat. Heat chili sauce and jelly in skillet, stirring constantly until jelly is melted. Add meatballs and stir well until thoroughly coated. Simmer uncovered until heated through.

Serve in chafing dish. These may be made ahead of time and frozen, if desired.

DEEP FRIED VEGETABLES (PAKORAS)

Yield: 40

Vegetables (eggplant,
   mushrooms, cauliflower,
   etc.)
1 cup sifted all-purpose flour or
   unsifted whole wheat flour
2 teaspoons ground coriander
2 teaspoons ground cumin
1 teaspoon black pepper,
   freshly ground
2 teaspoons ground celery
   seed
2 teaspoons salt
½ teaspoon baking powder
1⅓ cups water, or less

Prepare vegetables by cleaning and cutting in bite-sized pieces. Dry thoroughly. Combine remaining dry ingredients, and add water gradually to make batter. Dip vegetable pieces in batter, and deep fry until golden.

For eggplant: Pare, slice ¾ inch thick. Place in colander, sprinkle heavily with salt, and let drain 30 minutes. Dry with paper towel and cut into strips.

Appetizers

GOLDEN CHICKEN NUGGETS

Yield: 4 Dozen

4 whole chicken breasts, cut
   into 1-inch squares
½ cup butter, melted
½ cup fine dry bread crumbs
¼ cup grated Parmesan cheese
½ teaspoon salt
1 teaspoon dried thyme
1 teaspoon dried basil

Mix the dry ingredients. Dip chicken squares in melted butter and then into crumb mixture. Place in a single layer on ungreased baking sheets. Bake at 400°F for 10 minutes. Serve hot or cold.

ZUCCHINI APPETIZERS

Serves 4 to 6

3 cups zucchini, unpared, thinly
   sliced (about 4 small)
1 cup biscuit mix
½ cup finely chopped onion
½ cup grated Parmesan cheese
2 tablespoons parsley, fresh
½ teaspoon salt
½ teaspoon seasoned salt
½ teaspoon marjoram or
   oregano
Dash of pepper
1 small clove garlic, finely
   chopped
½ cup vegetable oil
4 eggs, slightly beaten

Mix all ingredients together, and spread in a greased 9 x 13-inch pan. Bake at 350°F for 25 minutes or until golden brown. Cut into bite-sized pieces, and let cool for a few minutes before serving.

These may be frozen, but do not cut first. Thaw and reheat, then cut.

SAUSAGE BALLS

Yield: 50

1 lb. well-seasoned ground
　　sausage
½ lb. sharp cheddar cheese,
　　grated
1½ cups flour
¼ teaspoon salt
1 teaspoon paprika
½ cup butter, melted

Form sausage into small balls, about ½ tablespoon each. Fry out most of the fat, browning on all sices (shake skillet every few minutes), and drain on absorbent paper. Combine grated cheese with dry ingredients. Mix in melted butter. Shape about 1 tablespoon of dough around each sausage ball. (Freeze at this point, if desired.) When ready to serve, place frozen balls on ungreased baking sheet. Bake at 400°F for 12 to 15 minutes. If not frozen, bake at 350°F for 8 to 10 minutes.

SEAFOOD MOUSSE

Serves 20

¾ cup minced onion
¾ cup minced celery
2 cans medium shrimp, or 1 can
　　shrimp and 1 package
　　frozen, thawed, crab meat:
　　12 to 14 oz. total, minced
1 can tomato soup: 10¾ oz.
5½ ounces cream cheese
1½ tablespoons gelatin
½ cup cold water
1 cup mayonnaise

Bring soup to boil; add cheese in chunks, and stir as cheese melts. Soften gelatin in water, then add to soup, stirring constantly. When the soup mixture has cooled, fold in vegetables, seafood, and mayonnaise. Refrigerate overnight in a lightly oiled mold covered with clear plastic wrap. Take out of refrigerator one-half hour before serving.
　Best with melba toast or lightly salted crackers.

Appetizers

NOVA SCOTIA SALMON MOLD

Yield: 3 Cups

1 envelope gelatin
¼ cup cold water
½ cup hot cream
8 ounces cream cheese, softened
1 cup sour cream
1 teaspoon Worcestershire sauce
Dash of Tabasco
2 tablespoons chopped green onions or chives
1 teaspoon lemon juice
1 tablespoon chopped parsley
1 tablespoon horseradish
1 cup Nova Scotia lox or smoked salmon, cut into ½-inch squares: ½ lb.
4 ounces red caviar
Fresh parsley

Soak gelatin in cold water; dissolve thoroughly in hot cream; cool. Mash cheese until smooth. Blend with sour cream, Worcestershire, Tabasco, and onion or chives. Stir into dissolved gelatin. Add lemon juice, parsley, salmon, and horseradish. Fold in caviar very carefully, so as not to break the globules. Pour into well-greased 3-cup mold. (A fish mold is attractive.) Refrigerate until congealed.

Serve on parsley-lined platter. Garnish with watercress and cherry tomatoes. Circle with cocktail rye, sliced thin. This mold may be made the day before serving.

Swiss
SNUFF BOX (incorporating a watch and musical automata) ca. 1825
gold, chased, engraved and enameled; pearls
Ruth Allison Lilly Watch Collection, 73.70.79

SHRIMP WITH MUSTARD SAUCE

Serves 8 to 10

2½ lbs. cooked shrimp
¼ cup finely chopped parsley
¼ cup finely chopped shallots
¼ cup tarragon vinegar
¼ cup wine vinegar
4 tablespoons Dijon mustard
2 teaspoons crushed red
    peppers
2 teaspoons salt
    Pepper, freshly ground

Place cooked shrimp in a large glass or ceramic bowl. Combine remaining ingredients and shake well in a jar, or mix in blender or processor. Pour over shrimp. Cover bowl and refrigerate several hours or overnight.

Serve on a bed of crisp lettuce, and pass with toothpicks, or serve as a first course at dinner with Italian or French bread. Hot!

BAKED SHRIMP DIP

Yield: 2 Cups

8 ounces cream cheese
1 can deveined shrimp: 4½ oz.
2 tablespoons minced onions
1 tablespoon milk
½ teaspoon horseradish
⅓ cup sliced almonds
¼ teaspoon salt
    Pepper

Mix ingredients well and bake in small casserole at 375°F for 15 minutes. Serve hot with raw vegetables or crackers.

May be prepared the day ahead, brought to room temperature, and baked as directed.

Appetizers

CRAB MEAT SPREAD

Serves 10 to 12

12 ounces cream cheese,
    softened
2 tablespoons mayonnaise
2 tablespoons Worcestershire
    sauce
1 teaspoon lemon juice
1 small onion, minced
1 garlic clove, minced
½ bottle chili sauce: 6 oz.
1 can crab meat, drained,
    minced, or frozen, thawed:
    6½ oz.
  Lemon juice
  Pepper
  Parsley, chopped

Blend cream cheese, mayonnaise, Worcestershire sauce, lemon juice, onion, and garlic. Spread in shallow serving dish. Spread chili sauce over cream cheese mixture. Top with crab meat, and sprinkle with lemon juice, pepper, and chopped parsley.
  Serve with your favorite crackers.

CAVIAR PÂTÉ

Serves 12

2 ounces black caviar or 1 jar:
    3 oz.
1 tablespoon lemon juice
1 envelope gelatin
¼ cup water
¼ cup mayonnaise
1 teaspoon Worcestershire
    sauce
1 teaspoon minced onion
  Salt
  Pepper
3 hard-cooked eggs, sieved

Marinate caviar in lemon juice and set aside. Dissolve gelatin in water. Combine with next six ingredients. Fold in caviar carefully by hand so as not to break eggs. Pour into a small mold. Chill overnight. Unmold and garnish with sour cream and parsley.

INDIANAPOLIS COLLECTS & COOKS

MOLDED LIVERWURST SPREAD

Serves 6 to 10

1 envelope gelatin
¼ cup cold water
1 can condensed beef
    consommé: 10½ oz.
8 ounces liverwurst
1 cup sour cream
3 tablespoons dry sherry
2 teaspoons Worcestershire
    sauce
¼ teaspoon ground nutmeg
¼ teaspoon dry mustard

Sprinkle the gelatin over cold water, and let stand for 5 minutes to soften. In a small pan heat the consommé to boiling. Remove from heat; add the gelatin mixture, and stir until the gelatin dissolves. Pour ½ cup of this mixture into bottom of an oiled 4-cup mold. Chill until firm. Mix remainder with the liverwurst, sour cream, sherry, Worcestershire sauce, nutmeg, and mustard until smooth. Pour on top of the congealed consommé, and chill until firm. Unmold.

Serve surrounded with chopped parsley and your favorite crackers. Will keep in the refrigerator for several days. Best made a day ahead. Can be frozen.

PÂTÉ MINIATURES

Serves 8 to 12

1 envelope gelatin
1 can condensed beef
    consommé: 10½ oz.
3 tablespoons water
4 stuffed olives, sliced
1 can liver pâté: 4½ oz.
1 can deviled ham: 4½ oz.
3 ounces cream cheese
1 teaspoon grated onion
    24 melba toast rounds

Soften gelatin in consommé in saucepan; heat until gelatin dissolves. Remove from heat and stir in water. Place olive slice in each of 24 tiny muffin pans. Spoon 1 teaspoon gelatin mixture into each. Chill 10 minutes until sticky firm. Blend liver pâté and deviled ham, cream cheese, onion, and ¼ cup gelatin mixture. Spoon 1 tablespoon over sticky-firm layer in each cup. Chill again until sticky firm. Spoon remaining gelatin mixture over each, dividing equally. Chill several hours. Remove from molds, place each on a melba toast round. Decorate serving platter with watercress.

Homemade melba toast: From thin-sliced bread cut rounds to size of pâté mixture. Butter lightly and bake 15 minutes at 350°F.

Appetizers

PÂTÉ DE FOIE À LA CRÈME

Serves 25 to 30

Chilled Crème
2 teaspoons gelatin
3 tablespoons water
6 ounces cream cheese, cut in chunks
1 can consommé, chilled: 13 oz.
1 tablespoon Madeira wine

Pâté
1 cup unsalted butter, divided
1 onion, peeled and quartered
1 teaspoon dry mustard
½ teaspoon salt
¼ teaspoon curry powder
¼ teaspoon ground cloves
⅛ teaspoon ground pepper
Dash cayenne pepper
1 lb. chicken livers
1 teaspoon gelatin
3 tablespoons water
2 tablespoons cognac or Madeira
½ cup whipping cream

Butter an 8-inch round cake pan. Line with wax paper, and butter paper. Sprinkle gelatin over water in small saucepan; dissolve over low heat. Cool. Add gelatin, cream cheese, chilled consommé, and wine to processor or blender, and mix until smooth. Pour cheese mixture into prepared pan. Cover with plastic wrap, and chill until firm.

Pâté: Melt ½ cup butter in skillet. Add onion, mustard, salt, curry, cloves, pepper, and cayenne. Cook and stir over medium heat until onion is tender. Add livers and cook until they are no longer pink. Process in blender until smooth. In small saucepan sprinkle gelatin over water and heat to dissolve.

Cool. Add cognac, cream, and the remaining ½ cup butter, cut in chunks, to the liver in the processor or blender. Add cooled gelatin, and blend until smooth. Remove plastic wrap from cheese base, and pour the liver mixture over it. Cover and chill several hours. To serve: invert on serving platter and garnish with pimiento, green pepper, etc.

The garnish may be arranged on the bottom of the cake pan before pouring in the cream mixture; trim with parsley or watercress. Serve with crackers or toast.

INDIANAPOLIS COLLECTS & COOKS

VERMOUTH LIVER PÂTÉ

Yield: 4½ Cups

1 cup minced onions
2 tablespoons rendered
  chicken fat
1 cup minced mushrooms
6 tablespoons rendered
  chicken fat
3 tablespoons flour
½ cup milk
½ lb. chicken livers, trimmed,
  rinsed, and drained
¼ lb. ground round
1 egg
1½ teaspoons salt
½ teaspoon pepper
2 hard-cooked eggs,
  finely chopped
2 tablespoons sweet
  Italian vermouth

Sauté onions in 2 tablespoons fat in skillet over medium heat for 10 minutes or until onions are transparent. Add mushrooms. Cook and stir for 3 minutes. Don't brown the mushrooms. Transfer the mixture to large bowl. Melt the 6 tablespoons fat over low heat. Add flour. Cook and stir 2 minutes. Add milk all at once. Cook and stir over medium heat until mixture thickens and separates, about 3 minutes. Stir this mixture into the onion and mushroom mixture.

Place livers, ground round, 1 egg, salt, and pepper in blender and cover. Blend until smooth, about 15 seconds. Stir liver mixture, chopped eggs, and vermouth into the mushroom-onion mixture. Heat oven to 350°F. Pour liver mixture into a 1½-quart casserole or loaf pan. Cover dish with double layer of aluminum foil. Set in larger shallow pan. Pour 1 inch boiling water in pan. Bake 45 minutes. Uncover and bake 1 hour longer. Refrigerate at least 6 hours. Unmold and garnish.

Appetizers

SOUPS AND SANDWICHES

MULLIGATAWNY

Serves 8

2½ lbs. chicken or chicken parts
8 cups chicken broth,
   canned or fresh
1 carrot, sliced
1 onion, quartered
1 large rib celery, chopped
3 sprigs parsley
1 bay leaf
6 tablespoons butter
1 medium onion, finely chopped
2 cloves garlic, minced
¼ cup flour
1 tablespoon curry powder
2 cups canned garbanzos and
   liquid
1 raw apple, peeled and
   chopped fine
Salt
Hot cooked rice
Lemon, thinly sliced

In soup kettle combine first seven ingredients. Bring to boil and skim. Lower heat to simmer, cover, and allow to cook until chicken is done, about 1 hour. Remove chicken, debone, dice, and set aside (discard bones). Strain broth through a fine sieve into a large bowl. Rinse soup pot, dry, and return to burner. Melt butter in pot; add chopped onion and garlic. Sauté until tender, stirring occasionally. With wooden spoon stir in flour and curry powder. Cook 3 to 4 minutes, stirring constantly. Slowly add chicken broth, beating with wire whisk to avoid lumping. Whirl garbanzos and liquid in blender, add to soup. Add chicken. Bring to a simmer, and stir in chopped apple. Taste for salt and adjust. Cook 10 minutes.

Serve in bowls, adding hot rice in center and lemon on the side.

LENTIL SOUP

Yield: 3 Quarts

1 lb. lentils
½ lb. bacon, diced
1 medium onion, diced
2 medium potatoes, diced
1 small carrot, diced
1 ham hock
   (or leftover ham bone)
3 quarts water
2 knockwurst
Salt
Pepper

Sort and rinse lentils. Cover with cold water, and soak overnight. Drain. In large soup pot sauté bacon until crisp. Add onion, potatoes, and carrot; and sauté until onions are golden. Add ham hock, water, and beans. Bring to boil and simmer, covered, for 4 hours. Remove ham hock. Dice meat from hock, and place back in pot. Add knockwurst. Simmer 30 minutes. Add salt and pepper. Remove knockwurst, peel and cut in small pieces.
Return to pot. Serve.

Taste improves as ingredients "sit." To reheat use VERY low heat. This recipe freezes well.

INDIANAPOLIS COLLECTS & COOKS   27

BRANDY CHEDDAR SOUP

Serves 6

¾ cup finely chopped carrots
⅔ cup finely chopped celery
⅓ cup finely chopped
   green onions
¼ cup melted butter
⅓ cup flour
 2 cups chicken broth
 2 cups half and half
¼ teaspoon salt
1½ cups shredded sharp
   cheddar cheese
 1 tablespoon brandy
   Chopped fresh parsley
   Croutons

Sauté vegetables in butter until soft, but not brown; blend in flour. Gradually stir in broth, then half and half. Cook stirring constantly, until mixture thickens and boils. Stir in salt, cheese, and brandy. Sprinkle with parsley and croutons.

NEW ENGLAND FISH CHOWDER

Serves 2 to 4

 1 lb. haddock fillets,
   partially thawed
 2 tablespoons chopped bacon
¼ cup chopped onion
 2 cups hot water
 1 cup cubed potatoes
 2 cups whole milk
¾ teaspoon salt
   Dash of pepper
   Chopped parsley

Cut the fillets in 1-inch cubes. Fry bacon until crisp and browned. Add onions and brown slightly. Add water and potatoes, and cook 10 minutes or until potatoes are partially tender. Add fish and simmer covered until fish can be flaked easily with a fork, about 10 minutes. Add milk, seasonings, and heat. Serve immediately with parsley sprinkled over the top.
   Serve with a salad for family supper.

Soups and Sandwiches

AVOCADO SOUP

Serves 6 to 8

3 avocados
3 cups chicken broth or bouillon
1½ cucumbers, peeled and sliced
    (approximately 2 cups)
¾ cups sour cream
3 tablespoons lemon juice
1½ teaspoons salt
    Dash of Tabasco
3 large tomatoes, peeled
    and diced

Purée avocados with all ingredients except tomatoes. Chill thoroughly. Garnish with diced tomatoes and serve.

CREOLE BEAN SOUP

Serves 8

1 lb. dry Great Northern beans
1 ham bone with some ham
8 cups water
1 cup chopped onions
1½ cups sliced carrots
½ cup diced green pepper
½ cup chopped celery
    with leaves
1 can tomatoes: 28 oz.
    (3½ cups)
    Salt
    Pepper

Wash beans and drain. Soak overnight. Combine beans, ham bone and water. Simmer over low heat for 1 hour. Add rest of ingredients except salt and pepper. Simmer another hour, until beans are tender. Add salt and pepper. Add more water if desired, but this is a thick hearty soup.

CHICKEN AVOCADO SOUP

Serves 6

4 cups chicken bouillon, cold
2 cups diced avocado
¼ cup lime juice
1 teaspoon salt
Freshly ground black pepper

Combine ingredients. Blend in a blender or with a rotary beater until smooth. Chill for at least 1 hour and serve.

HEARTY FALL VEGETABLE BEAN SOUP

Serves 8

6 cups water
1 cup Great Northern
    white beans
1 cup pinto beans
12 cups rich beef or
    chicken stock
1 large clove garlic
1 bay leaf
    Olive oil
1 cup chopped onion
1 cup chopped celery
1 cup green beans
1 cup chopped tomato
1 cup chopped carrots
1 cup chopped zucchini
1 cup lima beans or peas
1 cup broken spaghetti
    Parmesan cheese

Soak white beans and pinto beans in the water overnight; or bring to a boil, boil 2 minutes and soak 1 hour. Add the stock, garlic, and bay leaf. Simmer for 1 hour. In olive oil sauté the onion, celery, green beans, tomatoes, carrots, zucchini, and lima beans or peas until soft. Add to soup pot. Cook until beans are tender, at least 1 hour. Add the spaghetti and cook until tender, about 30 minutes.

Serve sprinkled with Parmesan cheese.

Soups and Sandwiches

BLACK BEAN SOUP

Serves 6 to 8

2 cups dry black turtle beans
4 beef bouillon cubes
1 bay leaf
1 tablespoon parsley
1 teaspoon paprika
2 tablespoons Worcestershire
   sauce
1 teaspoon sugar
2 teaspoons salt (optional)
¼ teaspoon pepper
1 teaspoon fines herbes
⅛ teaspoon cayenne pepper
⅓ lb. bacon, finely chopped
½ lb. ham, finely chopped
2 medium onions, chopped
1 clove garlic
1 stalk celery, chopped
1 green pepper, chopped
2 tablespoons each butter and
   flour (if needed for
   thickening)

Soak the beans overnight. Drain. Add water to beans to make 2 quarts. Combine in large kettle with bouillon cubes, bay leaf, parsley, paprika, Worcestershire sauce, sugar, salt (if needed), pepper, fines herbes, cayenne. Bring to boil, then simmer, covered. In a large skillet cook bacon. Add ham, onions, garlic, celery, and green pepper. Cook until tender. Add this to soup kettle. Cook at least 4 hours, covered. Before serving, correct seasoning, thicken if needed.

Serve with crumbled bacon, chives, sherry. Reheats well.

A hearty flavorful soup.

DECORATIVE ARTS SOCIETY
SPRING DINNER ON THE LILLY PAVILION TERRACE

Pâté de Foie à la Crème with Crackers
Hot Tomato Starter
Chester Cakes
Veal Marsala with Noodles
Spinach with Fresh Cream
Bibb Lettuce with Vinaigrette à l'Italienne
Maple Syrup Mousse
Lace Cookies

GREEN SOUP

Yield: 3 cups

½ cup diced green pepper
¼ cup chopped onion
1¼ cups chicken stock
1 pkg. frozen broccoli, chopped:
    10 oz., or fresh broccoli: 2 cups
½ cup buttermilk
1 cup half and half
⅛ teaspoon curry powder (more
    to taste)
  Salt
  Pepper

Simmer first four ingredients 20 minutes.
Purée in blender or food processor.
Transfer purée to pan. Add the rest of the ingredients, and heat over low temperature. Do not boil.
    Serve hot or delicious when served cold.

SLIM VEGETABLE SOUP

Serves 8 to 10

1 can tomato vegetable juice:
    46 oz.
2 zucchinis, quartered and
    sliced
4 carrots, pared and sliced
1 lb. mushrooms, sliced
4 ribs celery, sliced
1 onion, diced
1 small head cabbage,
    shredded
1 package frozen green beans:
    10 oz.
1 can tomatoes, cut up: 28 oz.
3 beef bouillon cubes
  Salt

Mix all ingredients in a large saucepan.
Bring to boil and cook slowly until vegetables are tender, about 15 minutes.
    This soup is good cold.

Soups and Sandwiches

Fedor Afanassiev, Russian, 1846-1920, workmaster for the firm of Peter Carl Fabergé, St. Petersburg branch
JAPONICA, ca. 1882-1914
chalcedony, nephrite, rose quartz; diamonds; gold
Gift of Mr. Edward E. Petri in memory of Frances Hélène Petri, 69.46.77

English (London)
SIDE TABLE, ca. 1760-1765
red and white pine, gessoed, carved and gilded; marble veneer; brass
Given anonymously, 78.151

Johann Joachim Kaendler, German, 1706-1775
Meissen, Germany
LOVERS WITH A BIRDCAGE, 1736
hard paste porcelain
Gift of Mr. and Mrs. John H. Bookwalter, 61.29

Peruvian (Paracas Necropolis) BURIAL WRAPPING, Pre-Columbian, 500 B.C.-200 A.D. wool plain weave embroidered with wool in stem stitch Gift of Mrs. A. W. S. Herrington and Niblack Textile Fund, 47.88

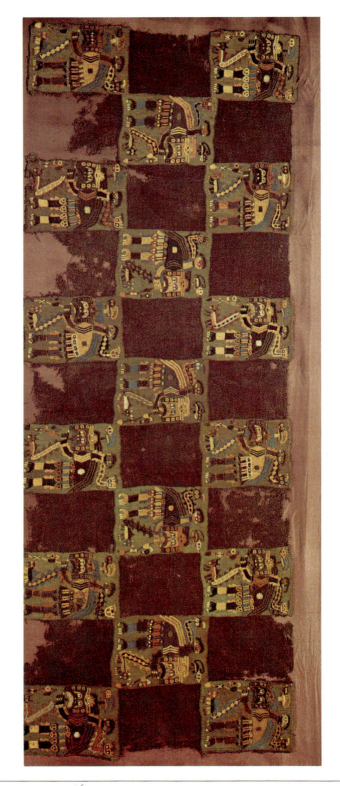

CREAM OF BROCCOLI SOUP

Serves 6

1 bunch fresh broccoli (about
  1½ lbs.) or 2 pkgs. frozen
  broccoli: 10½ oz. each
½ cup chopped onion
2 tablespoons butter
1 cup pared and diced potato
2 cans chicken stock: 13½ oz.
  each
¼ teaspoon salt
  Dash cayenne pepper
1 cup light cream
⅛ teaspoon ground nutmeg

Trim outer leaves and tough ends from broccoli. Separate stalks and cut into chunks. Parboil in salted water in large saucepan 5 minutes. Drain well. Sauté onion in butter in large saucepan until soft, but not brown, 5 minutes. Add potato, stock, salt, and cayenne. Heat to boiling, lower heat, and simmer 15 minutes. Add broccoli, reserving a few florets for garnish. Simmer 5 minutes longer or until vegetables are tender. Pour half of mixture into blender or food processor and blend until smooth. Repeat with other half. Pour mixture into saucepan when smooth. Add cream and nutmeg; bring to boil. Add more cream or milk if soup seems too thick. Garnish with florets.

SUMMER GREEN TWEED SOUP

Serves 8

1 quart buttermilk
2 teaspoons salt
½ green pepper, cut in squares
2 cucumbers, peeled, seeded, and sliced
¼ cup parsley, packed
6 scallions, with tops, cut in 1-inch pieces
1 teaspoon Worcestershire sauce
½ teaspoon celery seeds
¼ teaspoon dill weed or 1 teaspoon fresh dill, minced
Pepper

Place in blender 1 cup buttermilk, salt, green pepper, cucumbers, parsley, and onions. Blend until vegetables are chopped fine. Pour into tureen and add the remaining buttermilk, Worcestershire sauce, celery seeds, dill, and pepper. Chill soup and serve garnished with paper-thin slices of unpared cucumber.

Good recipe for dieters.

GAZPACHO

Serves 8

6 cups tomato juice
2 tablespoons olive oil
2 to 3 tablespoons lemon juice
1 cup beef broth
½ cup finely minced onion
3 tomatoes, finely minced
2 cups finely minced celery
½ green pepper, finely minced
2 cucumbers, seeded, finely minced
1 teaspoon salt
¼ teaspoon pepper
Dash of Tabasco

Combine all ingredients and mix well. Chill for several hours to blend flavors.

Serve with one or several side dishes of additional finely chopped onion, tomatoes, celery, pepper, cucumber, or croutons. May use blender or food processor to chop vegetables, but be sure they are minced, not puréed. Nice to serve before a meal of fish, green vegetable, tossed salad, and lemon dessert.

Soups and Sandwiches

BORSCHT WITH SOUR CREAM

Serves 8

1 cup canned beets with juice
1 medium onion, chopped
3 kosher dill pickles, chopped
½ cup dill pickle juice
1 tablespoon dill weed
  Ground black pepper
1 teaspoon garlic salt
1 teaspoon monosodium
  glutamate (MSG)
1 teaspoon liquid Maggi
1 drop Tabasco
1 can tomato juice: 46 oz.
1 cup julienne beets
6 hard-cooked eggs, sliced
  Yogurt or sour cream

Place first ten ingredients in blender or food processor bowl. Blend on medium speed until finely puréed. Place in serving bowl, and add the tomato juice, julienne beets, and sliced eggs. Stir and chill several hours. Serve with scoops of plain yogurt or sour cream.

Sprinkle with chopped parsley or dill, and serve with a thin rye crisp. May be strained and served over ice with vodka as a Bloody Russian. Keeps beautifully in the refrigerator.

CORN CHOWDER

Serves 6

½ cup chopped bacon
3 tablespoons chopped onion
½ cup chopped celery
3 tablespoons chopped
  green pepper
1 cup peeled and diced potato
2 cups water
½ teaspoon salt
¼ teaspoon paprika
½ bay leaf
3 tablespoons flour
½ cup milk
1½ cups hot milk
2 cups whole kernel corn

Sauté bacon slowly until lightly brown. Add onion, celery, and green pepper; and sauté until golden brown. Add potatoes, water, salt, paprika, and bay leaf. Cook until potatoes are tender, about 45 minutes. Blend flour and ½ cup milk, bring to boiling point, and add to above. Then add hot milk and corn. Heat, but do not boil the soup. Serve with chopped parsley on top.

INDIANAPOLIS COLLECTS & COOKS

CRÈME MUSHROOM OLGA

Serves 6 to 8

½ cup butter
8 cups (about 6 bunches)
   scallions, coarsely chopped
1 teaspoon salt
½ teaspoon white pepper
2 tablespoons flour
5 cups white veal or
   chicken stock, heated
½ lb. mushrooms,
   finely chopped
1¼ cups light cream
   or half and half
¼ lb. mushrooms, thinly sliced
   Whipped cream
   Salt
   Cayenne

Melt butter and mix with the scallions in heavy 4-quart soup pot, not aluminum. Season with salt and pepper, and simmer covered over moderate heat for ten minutes. Remove pan from heat, and stir in 2 tablespoons flour. Add heated stock and return to heat. Bring to a boil, reduce heat, and simmer 10 minutes. Turn off heat and add mushrooms. (Can be chopped in food processor.) Process the soup into a coarse texture. Return to the stove, and add 1¼ cups light cream or half and half. Correct seasoning to taste. Reheat and just before serving add thinly sliced raw mushrooms. Top each serving with 1 tablespoon whipped cream and a pinch of salt and cayenne.

CHILLED MUSHROOM-SHRIMP BISQUE

Serves 6 to 8

1 lb. fresh mushrooms
1½ cups water
1 teaspoon salt
1 small onion, peeled and
   quartered
¼ cup butter
¼ cup flour
1½ teaspoons salt
   Dash pepper
2½ cups milk
½ cup whipping cream
2 cups cooked shrimp

Rinse mushrooms and cut off tips of stems. Slice in food processor or by hand. Combine mushrooms, water, and 1 teaspoon salt in medium saucepan. Cover and simmer 10 minutes. Drain, reserving liquid and set both aside. Chop onion medium fine in food processor or by hand. Melt butter in saucepan and add onion. Sauté until tender. Add drained mushrooms. Blend in flour and 1½ teaspoons salt and pepper. Cook and stir until bubbly. Add mushroom liquid and milk. Cook and stir until mixture comes to a boil and is smooth and thickened. Remove from heat and stir in whipping cream. Chop shrimp coarsely in food processor or by hand and add to mushroom-cream mixture. Cover and chill thoroughly.

   A dash of sherry may be added when served.

Soups and Sandwiches

William Merritt Chase, American, 1849-1916
LADY IN WHITE, The artist's daughter, Alice Dieudonnee
oil on canvas, 29 x 19 inches
Gift of Mrs. Albert Metzger in memory of her husband, 45.241

FRENCH ONION SOUP

Serves 6

4 large onions
¼ cup butter
1 tablespoon flour
6 cups beef consommé (or
    water or a mixture of the
    two)
  French bread, sliced and
    toasted
  Gruyère cheese, grated

Peel and thinly slice onions; separate into rings. Heat butter in large saucepan and add onions. Cook very gently over low heat, stirring constantly with wooden spoon, until rings are an even golden brown. Sprinkle with flour, blending well. Gradually add consommé, and stir constantly until soup boils. Lower heat, cover the pan, and simmer gently for 20 minutes. Taste for seasoning, and serve in heated soup tureen or in individual tureens, each containing bread heaped with cheese.

Soup may also be served gratinée. Half fill an oven-proof casserole with toasted French bread slices covered with grated cheese. Pour soup over the toast. Top with more cheese, and put under broiler or in hot oven until brown and sizzling.

CREAM OF SORREL

Yield: 8 cups

1 cup rich chicken broth
1 can condensed cream of
  chicken soup
1 can condensed potato soup
1 cup or more sorrel, finely cut
  (spinach may be
  substituted)
3 tablespoons butter
1 cup heavy cream
2 cups half and half
  Salt
  Pepper

Combine the chicken broth with the cream of chicken and potato soups. Wilt the sorrel (or spinach) in a skillet with the butter. Add to the soups. Heat mixture just to the boiling point. Cool slightly and add the creams. Add salt and pepper if necessary. Chill for at least 12 hours. May be served cold or reheated gently to be served hot.

If you wish to serve this as a first course in a goblet, put the soups and sorrel through a blender before heating and adding the creams. This is delightful cold in summer for an elegant picnic or with sandwiches for lunch. If using spinach, add 1 tablespoon lemon juice to more closely approximate sorrel.

SPRING SCALLION SOUP

Serves 4

2 cups scallions, chopped
   (about 2 bunches, including
   green tops)
1 clove garlic
3 tablespoons butter
2 tablespoons flour
4 cups chicken bouillon, heated
  Salt
¼ teaspoon white pepper
1 egg yolk, lightly beaten
¼ cup cream
  Whipped cream
  Chopped chives

Stew the chopped scallions and garlic in the butter over a low flame until they are tender but not brown. Stir in flour. Add hot chicken bouillon gradually, stirring continuously. Simmer gently for 30 minutes. Taste for salt. Add pepper. Strain soup through a fine sieve or process 30 seconds. Just before serving stir in the egg yolk beaten with the cream and a little of the hot soup. Garnish each portion with a dollop of whipped cream, and sprinkle with finely chopped chives.

SUNCHOKE PURÉE

Serves 4 to 6

1 lb Jerusalem artichokes
   (Sunchokes)
2 tablespoons lemon juice
2 tablespoons butter
1 slice onion (2 tablespoons)
1 cup cold water
¼ teaspoon mace
2 cups scalded milk
1 teaspoon salt
⅛ teaspoon pepper
½ cup cream, whipped
2 tablespoons finely chopped nuts
  Paprika

Wash and pare artichokes and slice into cold water. Add juice of lemon and let stand 15 minutes. Drain. Melt butter, add artichokes and onion. Cook 5 minutes without browning. Add 1 cup cold water, mace, and cook until tender. Purée in blender. Reheat and add scalded milk, salt, and pepper. Garnish with whipped cream to which the nuts have been added and sprinkle with paprika.

Soups and Sandwiches

HOT TOMATO STARTER

Serves 8

1 can tomato juice: 46 oz.
1 can condensed beef
    consommé: 10½ oz.
1 teaspoon grated onion
1 teaspoon horseradish
    Dash of pepper
1 teaspoon Worcestershire
    sauce
1 lemon, sliced and seeded
    Whole cloves

In a saucepan combine juice, consommé, onion, horseradish, pepper, and Worcestershire sauce. Heat, stirring constantly.
Serve with lemon slices studded with cloves floating in each cup.

FRESH TOMATO SOUP

Yield: 4 to 5 Quarts

3 quarts sliced ripe tomatoes
6 onions, thinly sliced
8 tablespoons sugar
    Few sprigs parsley
40 whole cloves
4 teaspoons salt
½ teaspoon pepper
6 tablespoons butter
6 tablespoons cornstarch
½ cup water
2 quarts milk
    Whipped cream

Combine the first seven ingredients in a large saucepan. Bring to a boil and cook until ingredients are well cooked. Strain through food mill. Add the butter and stir until melted. Mix the cornstarch with the water, and add to the tomato mixture. Add the milk and heat thoroughly, stirring well.
Serve piping hot with a dollop of whipped cream on top. Also good cold.

TOMATO SOUP

Serves 6 to 8

½ cup butter
2 tablespoons olive oil
2 cups thinly sliced onion
2 sprigs fresh thyme or ½
    teaspoon dried thyme
4 basil leaves, chopped or ½
    teaspoon dried basil
 Salt to taste
 Freshly ground pepper to
    taste
2½ lbs. (5 cups) fresh ripe
    tomatoes, cored or 2 lb.
    can tomatoes (Italian style)
3 tablespoons tomato paste
¼ cup flour
3¾ cups fresh or canned
    chicken stock
1 teaspoon sugar
1 cup heavy cream
¼ cup butter (optional)

Heat ½ cup butter in a kettle and add olive oil. Add the onion, thyme, basil, salt, and freshly ground pepper. Cook, stirring occasionally, until onion is wilted. Add tomatoes and tomato paste and stir to blend. Simmer 10 minutes. Place the flour in small mixing bowl; add 5 tablespoons of chicken broth, stirring to blend. Stir this into tomato mixture. Add remaining chicken broth, and simmer 30 minutes, stirring frequently to make sure the soup does not stick, scorch, or burn. Put through finest sieve or food mill or purée in food processor. Return to heat and add sugar and cream. Simmer, stirring occasionally, about 5 minutes. Add remaining butter, swirling it around in the soup. This butter may be omitted, if desired.

The soup may be frozen after being puréed, but before adding the cream.

Soups and Sandwiches

SWISS PUMPKIN SHELL SUPPER

Serves 6 to 8

6 slices bread, cubed
1 well-formed pumpkin,
   with stem: 6 lb.
1 tablespoon oil
6 ounces Swiss cheese, grated
4 cups half and half
1 teaspoon salt
¼ teaspoon pepper
¼ teaspoon nutmeg
¼ teaspoon curry powder
2 teaspoons chopped onion

Toast bread cubes in 450°F oven for 5 minutes. Wash and dry pumpkin. Cut off top one-fourth down from top. Clean out fibers and seeds. Scrape well. Oil outside and pumpkin top. Place pumpkin on heavy pie plate. Alternately layer the bread cubes and cheese into the pumpkin filling three-fourths of the space, finishing with a layer of cheese. Combine the half and half, salt, pepper, nutmeg, curry powder, and onion. Pour over bread and cheese to cover adequately. Place cap on. Bake at 350°F 2 hours, stirring occasionally. Done when thickened and pumpkin meat is tender. Remove cap and ladle thickened custard and pumpkin pulp into soup dishes.

It's a soup served in its own tureen. Delicious! Fun!

HOT CALIFORNIA CHICKEN SALAD SANDWICH

Serves 6

3 cups diced cooked chicken
2 hard cooked eggs, cut up
½ cup canned sliced
   mushrooms, drained
¼ cup sliced stuffed olives
½ cup mayonnaise
12 slices thin-sliced white bread,
   crust removed
1 can cream of chicken soup:
   10½ oz.
1 cup sour cream
1 cup grated cheddar cheese

Combine first five ingredients, and mix well. Spread on 6 slices of bread. Cover with the remaining slices, and place in a baking dish. Combine the soup and sour cream, and spread over the sandwiches. Refrigerate overnight. Bake at 325°F for 20 minutes. Add cheese and bake until cheese melts.

CHICKEN ROQUEFORT SANDWICH FILLING

Yield: 3½ Cups

Roquefort Cheese Sauce
  8 ounces cream cheese
½ pint coffee cream
  4 ounces Roquefort cheese,
    crumbled
  3 drops Tabasco
   Salt to taste, very little
Filling
  3 cups chicken, chopped, not
    ground
  1 lb. bacon, diced, fried crisp,
    and crumbled

Mix all sauce ingredients together until fairly smooth and blended. Combine chicken and bacon, and add only enough Roquefort cheese sauce to make a good spreading consistency. Mix and refrigerate until ready to use. Before using, you may need to add a very small amount of cream since this mixture does thicken with chilling.

This mixture can be frozen. Use on your favorite bread, or stuff a tomato.

Soups and Sandwiches

CAULIFLOWER SOUP

Serves 6

- 1 head cauliflower, broken into florets
- ¼ cup chopped onion
- 4 tablespoons butter
- ¼ cup flour
- 3 cups chicken broth
- 2 cups milk
- 1 teaspoon Worcestershire sauce
- 1 teaspoon lemon juice
- 4 ounces cheddar cheese, grated; or fresh Parmesan, grated
- Salt
- White pepper

Cook cauliflower in salted water until tender, about 10 to 15 minutes. Strain, chop coarsely. Sauté onions in butter until tender. Blend in flour; add chicken broth, milk, and Worcestershire sauce. Cook until thick, stirring occasionally. Add cauliflower and heat. *Do not boil.* Add lemon juice just before serving. Garnish with shredded cheese, chives, chopped parsley, or paprika.

Paul Manship, American, 1885-1966
RAPE OF EUROPA
bronze
Gift of Lucy M. Taggart in memory of her brother, Thomas D. Taggart, 50.30

TUNA SWISS SPECIAL

Serves 6

1 can tuna, drained: 7 oz.
¼ cup chopped stuffed
  green olives
¼ cup chopped pecans
  Mayonnaise
6 French bread slices
  Butter
  Tomato slices
  Swiss cheese slices

Combine tuna, olives, nuts, and enough mayonnaise to moisten. Spread bread slices with butter; top with tomato slices, and broil 2 to 3 minutes. Cover with tuna mixture and cheese. Broil until cheese melts.

This simple and very good sandwich makes a hit with teenagers.

DENVER BRUNCH SANDWICH

Serves 6

½ cup mayonnaise
6 eggs
⅓ cup milk
½ lb. bacon, cooked and
  crumbled
½ cup chopped pimiento
¼ teaspoon salt
  Dash of pepper
6 green pepper rings

Beat eggs and milk into mayonnaise. Add the crumbled bacon, pimiento, salt, and pepper. Pour into a greased 8-inch square pan. Divide pepper rings over mixture to form divisions. Set in a pan of hot water. Bake at 350°F for 35 minutes or until set. Cut into squares and serve. This will wait in the oven for about 20 minutes after you shut off heat.

For brunch, serve with lettuce and tomato on toast slices spread with mayonnaise and garnish with bacon curls.

Soups and Sandwiches

BAKED TURKEY SANDWICHES

Serves 4

Mushroom Sauce
1 can mushroom soup,
    undiluted: 10½ oz.
¼ cup dry sherry
Sandwiches
8 slices toast
    Sliced cooked turkey or
      chicken
8 slices bacon, cooked crisp
½ cup grated cheddar cheese
    Paprika

Mix soup and sherry to make sauce. Place 2 slices toast side by side in each of four shallow, oval individual baking dishes. Spread toast with some of the mushroom sauce. Top with sliced turkey or chicken, and the crisp bacon slices. Distribute remaining mushroom sauce over sandwiches, sprinkle with grated cheese, and dust with paprika. Bake at 450°F for 10 minutes or until bubbly. Serve at once.

If more convenient, arrange and bake sandwiches in one large shallow baking pan, then carefully remove them to heated plates.

BARBECUED BEEF

Serves 16

2 tablespoons oil
4 lbs. chuck roast
2 cups beef broth
2 cups chopped onion
½ cup butter
4 tablespoons brown sugar
4 tablespoons vinegar
2 tablespoons dry mustard
1 bottle ketchup: 20 oz.
6 tablespoons Worcestershire
    sauce
12 drops Tabasco
    Pepper
    Salt

Brown meat in oil, and simmer in beef broth about 3 hours or until roast shreds. While roast simmers, mix together remaining ingredients. Simmer for two hours, or until thick. Add shredded beef and simmer a little longer to blend flavors. Serve on hamburger buns. This may be done in a crockpot.

To shred roast, remove from broth and scrape with fork.

INDIANAPOLIS COLLECTS & COOKS

BUSINESS UNIT GROUP SUNDAY LUNCHEON
IN THE FESLER MEMBERS' ROOM

 Curried Chicken Salad
Little Loaves with Herbs
Fresh Fruit and Cookies

CREAMY CELERY SPINACH SOUP

Serves 6

2 cups chopped celery
1 cup diced onions
1 package chopped spinach, cooked and drained: 10 oz.
1 can chicken stock or homemade chicken stock: 10½ oz.
1 cup cream style cottage cheese
2 cups milk
½ teaspoon salt
⅛ teaspoon pepper
½ cup sour cream

Combine celery, onion, spinach, and chicken broth. Simmer, covered, until tender (about 20 minutes). Purée in blender or food processor with cottage cheese. Return to saucepan. Add remaining ingredients except sour cream. Heat. Serve with sour cream garnish. May also be served chilled.

CRAB SANDWICHES

Serves 6

1 can crab meat, flaked: 6½ oz.
1 cup diced cheddar cheese
¼ cup finely chopped celery
½ teaspoon grated onion
½ cup mayonnaise
3 tablespoons chili sauce
6 hamburger buns

Combine filling ingredients; mix well. Split and butter buns. Spread crab mixture on buns. Wrap buns in foil, and bake at 325°F for 20 minutes. May be frozen—add 20 minutes to baking time.

Soups and Sandwiches

Edward Hopper, American, 1882-1967
NEW YORK, NEW HAVEN AND HARTFORD, 1931
oil on canvas, 32 x 50 inches
Emma Harter Sweetser Fund, 32.177

INDIANAPOLIS COLLECTS & COOKS

Winslow Homer, American, 1836-1910
THE BOAT BUILDERS, 1873
oil on mahogany panel, 6 x 10¼ inches
Martha Delzell Memorial Fund, 54.10

John Henry Twachtman, American, 1853-1902
A SUMMER DAY, ca. 1900
oil on canvas, 25 x 30⅛ inches
John Herron Fund, 07.3

Joshua Shaw, American, 1776-1860
THE PIONEERS, ca. 1838
oil on canvas, 12 x 27 inches
James E. Roberts and Emma Harter Sweetser Funds, 79.328

BRUNCH, LUNCH, AND SUPPER

CHEESE SOUFFLÉ

Serves 4 to 5

4 tablespoons butter
4 tablespoons flour
½ teaspoon salt
¼ teaspoon dry mustard
¼ teaspoon cayenne pepper
1 cup milk
1 cup shredded sharp cheese
   (cheddar)
3 egg yolks, well beaten
3 egg whites, beaten stiff with
   ¼ teaspoon cream of tartar

Melt butter and remove from heat. Blend in flour, salt, mustard, and pepper. Stir in milk; bring to boil, stirring constantly. Boil one minute; stir in cheese. Remove from heat; stir in well-beaten egg yolks. Fold in stiffly beaten egg whites. Pour into 1½-quart round casserole; set casserole in a pan of hot water which is deep enough to surround it well. Bake at 350°F for 50 to 60 minutes until puffed and golden brown. Serve immediately.

PRESNUTZ

Serves 8

½ cup butter
1 lb. Monterey Jack cheese,
   grated
1 lb. ricotta cheese, crumbled
¼ lb. feta cheese, crumbled
1 cup flour
2 cups milk
7 to 8 eggs

Melt butter in a 9 x 11-inch baking dish. Sprinkle the three cheeses into dish. Beat together the flour, milk, and eggs. Pour over the cheese. Bake at 350°F for 45 minutes, 325°F if using glass baking dish. Cheeses can be combined in dish and refrigerated; flour, eggs, and milk can be combined and refrigerated separately, then all combined just when ready to bake.

Can be reheated, but texture seems slightly heavier.

BRUNCH EGGS

Serves 6 to 8

8 slices white bread
1 lb. bacon
½ lb. fresh mushrooms, sliced
1 cup chopped onions
¾ lb. sharp cheddar cheese, shredded
9 eggs, slightly beaten
2 cups milk
¾ teaspoon dry mustard
¾ teaspoon salt
1 teaspoon Worcestershire sauce

Butter bread, remove crusts, and cut in cubes. Fry bacon and crumble. Sauté mushrooms. Layer in large pan, alternating bread, bacon, mushrooms, onions, and cheese. Mix remaining ingredients; pour over layers. Refrigerate overnight. Remove one hour before baking at 350°F for 60 minutes.

CREAMED EGGS

Serves 4

6 hard-boiled eggs, quartered
½ cup ham, diced
½ lb. mushrooms, sautéed in butter
1½ cups thick Cream Sauce
¼ cup sherry
½ cup grated Swiss cheese
Cream Sauce
3 tablespoons butter
4 tablespoons flour
1¼ cups milk

Place eggs in bottom of 8 x 8-inch baking dish; add ham and mushrooms. Make cream sauce by stirring flour into melted butter; add milk gradually and stir over low heat until smooth. Cool slightly. Stir in sherry. Pour over top of eggs, mushrooms, and ham. Cover with cheese. Bake at 350°F for 45 minutes.

This may be made the day before and refrigerated. If doubled, bake slightly longer.

Brunch, Lunch and Supper

CURRIED EGGS WITH SHRIMP SAUCE

Serves 8 for Lunch—4 for Brunch or Supper

8 hard-boiled eggs
½ teaspoon salt
⅛ teaspoon Worcestershire
   sauce
½ teaspoon curry powder
¼ teaspoon paprika
¼ teaspoon dry mustard
1½ tablespoons lemon juice
  2 to 3 tablespoons sour cream
Cheese-Shrimp Sauce
  3 tablespoons butter
  3 tablespoons flour
  2 cups light cream
½ teaspoon salt
  Pepper
  1 teaspoon Worcestershire
    sauce
  1 cup shredded sharp
    cheddar cheese
½ lb. cooked shrimp or 2 cans
    shrimp: 4½ oz. each

Cut eggs in half lengthwise, and scoop out yolks. Mash yolks with salt, Worcestershire sauce, curry powder, paprika, mustard, lemon juice, and sour cream. Fill egg halves with this mixture, and press together. Place in a greased, 8-inch-square baking dish. Pour the Cheese-Shrimp Sauce over the deviled eggs.

Cheese-Shrimp Sauce: Melt butter over low heat in medium pan. Add flour and stir until well combined. Add cream slowly and stir constantly until sauce thickens. Add salt, pepper, Worcestershire sauce, and cheese; and stir until smooth. Cut the shrimp into pieces, and add to the sauce.

SHRIMP AND SHELL SALAD

Serves 4 to 6

2 cups medium macaroni
    shells: 8 oz.
1 lb. cooked shrimp, cut in half
1½ cups green beans, cooked
    crisp and drained
¼ cup sliced scallions or 1 small
    purple onion, cut in rings
2 tablespoons pimiento,
    chopped
⅓ cup vegetable oil
⅓ cup lemon juice
1 garlic clove, minced
1 teaspoon salt
½ teaspoon thyme
¼ teaspoon oregano

Cook macaroni in boiling, salted water until tender. Drain and rinse with cold water. Set aside. Mix shrimp, beans, onion, and pimiento in large bowl. Combine remaining ingredients for dressing, and pour over shrimp. Mix well; add macaroni, and mix again. Cover and refrigerate.

Prepare early in the day so ingredients are well chilled and flavors can blend. Serve in zucchini or cucumber boats for lunch.

PASHA

Serves 6 to 8

4 tablespoons butter
4 tablespoons light brown sugar
2 cups small curd
    cottage cheese, drained
2 egg yolks
¼ teaspoon vanilla
⅔ cup raisins
⅔ cup ground, unblanched
    almonds
  Salt
  Ham, thinly sliced

Cream butter and sugar. Add the remaining ingredients, and mix well. Form into a mold with hands or gently press into a decorative mold. Refrigerate overnight. Unmold on tray or platter just before serving. Circle Pasha with thin slices of ham.

Fresh strawberries with powdered sugar or fresh fruit kabobs accompany this very nicely.

POZ NOZ

Serves 4

2 lb. small curd cottage cheese
1 package frozen, chopped
    spinach, thawed and
    drained: 10 oz.
6 eggs
⅓ cup flour
½ lb. sharp cheese, grated
¼ cup melted butter
½ cup chopped onion
1 teaspoon salt
⅛ teaspoon nutmeg, optional
  Grated sharp cheese

Combine and mix all ingredients. When thoroughly mixed, pour into a 1½-quart casserole. Sprinkle grated cheese generously on top, and bake at 350°F for 1 hour, or until a knife blade will come out clean after being inserted.

May be frozen.

Brunch, Lunch and Supper

MUSHROOM STROGANOFF

Serves 20

4 lbs. mushrooms, sliced
3½ to 4 onions, sliced
¾ to 1 bunch celery, sliced
6 to 8 tablespoons butter
6 to 8 cups sour cream
1 teaspoon pepper
1 tablespoon salt
1 tablespoon basil
¼ teaspoon nutmeg
1 teaspoon garlic powder
1 teaspoon thyme
1 teaspoon dill
Paste
  1 tablespoon dry mustard
  ½ teaspoon sugar
  1 teaspoon salt
  Water

Sauté the mushrooms, onions and celery in butter. Add sour cream and spices. Make a paste of the dry mustard, sugar, and salt mixed with enough water to make it thick. Add to the mushroom mixture, and serve on cooked wild or whole grain rice.

A delicious vegetarian entrée.

SWEDISH CREAMED MUSHROOMS

Serves 4

½ lb. mushrooms
2 tablespoons butter
1 tablespoon chopped onion
1 teaspoon salt
  Pepper
1 teaspoon lemon juice
2 tablespoons flour
½ cup cream
½ cup milk
½ teaspoon Worcestershire sauce
1 tablespoon sherry or
    dry vermouth, optional

Slice mushrooms lengthwise. Melt butter in saucepan. Add mushrooms, onions, salt, pepper, and lemon juice. Cover and simmer for 5 minutes. Stir in flour. Gradually add cream, milk, and Worcestershire sauce. Cook, stirring until smooth and thickened. Stir in wine and remove from heat.

Serve on toast points or as filling in omelet or in pastry shells.

ONION PIE

Serves 6 to 8

Pastry
1½ cups sifted flour
1 teaspoon salt
1½ teaspoons caraway seeds
½ cup shortening
2 to 3 tablespoons water
Filling
3 cups thinly sliced onions
3 tablespoons melted butter
½ cup milk
1½ cups sour cream
1 teaspoon salt
2 eggs, well beaten
3 tablespoons flour
4 bacon slices, fried crisp

Combine flour, salt, and caraway seeds. Add shortening. Cut into flour until mixture resembles coarse cornmeal. Stir in water lightly with a fork. Stir until mixture adheres and follows fork around bowl. Turn onto floured board; roll to ⅛-inch thickness. Fit into a 10-inch pie pan. Flute edge. Bake at 425°F for about 10 minutes or until lightly browned.

Filling: Sauté onions in butter until lightly browned. Spoon into pastry shell. Add milk, 1¼ cups sour cream, and salt to eggs. Blend 3 tablespoons flour with remaining ¼ cup sour cream. Combine with egg mixture. Pour over onions. Bake ar 325°F for 30 minutes, or until firm in center. Garnish with crisp bacon slices.

SKILLET SPLIT PEA DINNER

Serves 4

1 cup split peas
2 cups water
1 teaspoon salt
½ teaspoon basil
Dash pepper
1½ cups cubed cooked ham
1 medium green pepper, sliced
in thin strips

In a skillet over medium high heat, combine split peas, water, salt, basil, and pepper; bring to boil. Reduce heat to low, cover, and simmer 35 minutes. Add ham and green pepper; cover and cook 10 minutes longer or until peas are tender. Add more water if it seems too thick.

SPINACH AND HAM ROLL-UPS

Serves 18 for Luncheon—9 for Dinner

1 package frozen, chopped
spinach; thawed and very
well drained: 10 oz.
1 can cream of celery soup:
10¾ oz.
1 cup sour cream
1½ tablespoons Dijon-style
mustard
1½ cups cooked rice
1 cup small curd
cottage cheese
2 eggs, well beaten
⅓ cup onion, finely chopped
¼ cup flour
18 slices packaged boiled ham
¾ cup fine bread crumbs
3 tablespoons melted butter
Paprika

Place the thawed spinach in a colander or sieve, and press out the remaining water until dry. Set aside. In a small bowl mix together the soup, sour cream, and mustard. In a medium bowl combine ½ cup of soup mixture with the spinach, rice, cottage cheese, eggs, onion, and flour; mix well. Press the ham slices between paper towels to remove the moisture. Place about 2 heaping tablespoons of the spinach mixture on each ham slice. Roll up and place close together, seam side down, in a baking dish about 11 x 7 inches. Spoon the rest of the soup mixture over the ham rolls, top with crumbs that have been mixed with melted butter, and sprinkle with paprika. Bake, uncovered, at 350°F for 30 minutes or until sauce is bubbly. Remove from oven and let stand 10 minutes before serving.

INDIANAPOLIS COLLECTS & COOKS

SPINACH CRÊPES WITH HAM AND CHEESE

Yield: 24 Crêpes

Crêpes
1 package frozen chopped
    spinach
½ cup water
½ cup milk
2 eggs
2 tablespoons melted butter
1 cup flour
¼ teaspoon salt
Filling
24 thin baked ham slices: 1 oz.
    each
  Swiss cheese
  Topping
  Melted butter
  Grated Parmesan cheese

Cook spinach as directed. Cool, but do not drain. Put spinach into blender and blend until smooth. Add ½ cup water and remaining ingredients, and blend for 1 minute. Let batter stand for 2 hours or overnight in refrigerator. Very lightly butter a 6-inch crêpe pan. Cook as you would any crêpes. To assemble, lay a 1-ounce paper-thin slice of baked ham on crêpe and top with a finger of Swiss cheese. Roll crêpes like a jelly roll, and arrange in an oven-proof gratin dish. Brush well with melted butter, and cover with Parmesan cheese. Heat at 400°F for 10 minutes or until cheese has melted and tops are bubbling and lightly glazed.

Crêpes may be cooked ahead and frozen, separated by pieces of wax paper.

BLACK-EYED PEAS AND POT LIKKER

Serves 6 to 10

1 lb. black-eyed peas
1½ quarts water
1 lb. ham pieces or a
    meaty ham bone
1 cup grated carrots
1 cup chopped onions
1 teaspoon thyme
¼ cup chopped parsley
  Salt
  Pepper

Soak peas overnight in the cold water, or soak 6 hours in warm water. Put on to cook with same water. Add remaining ingredients and simmer 2 to 4 hours, adding more water if necessary.

Serve with corn bread and cole slaw.

Brunch, Lunch and Supper

NOODLES WITH PESTO

Serves 8

2 cups fresh basil leaves or 2
    cups fresh parsley and 2
    teaspoons dried basil
¼ cup olive oil
2 tablespoons pine nuts
2 cloves garlic, lightly crushed
2 tablespoons parsley
1 teaspoon salt
½ cup Parmesan cheese
2 tablespoons Romano cheese
3 tablespoons butter, softened
8 ounces noodles, cooked

Put basil, olive oil, pine nuts, garlic, parsley, and salt in blender; and mix. (Can be frozen at this point.) When the ingredients are evenly blended, pour into a bowl; and beat in the two cheeses. Beat in the softened butter. Add the cooked noodles and 1 tablespoon of the hot water in which the noodles were boiled. Blend with the sauce, and add more cheese, if desired.

Excellent with spinach noodles, but any pasta may be used. You'll want to plant some basil after you try this great pesto sauce.

PASTA FETTUCCINI

Serves 6 as Side Dish—4 as Entrée

3 cups unbleached flour
1 teaspoon salt
4 eggs
1 tablespoon olive oil
2 tablespoons water

Combine ingredients in food processor. Allow to rest ½ to 1 hour, covered tightly with plastic wrap. Cut into 4 pieces, then cut each of those into 3 pieces. Using pasta machine, put through lowest setting several times, dusting with flour. Gradually tighten the bars until at desired thickness, rolling dough through each setting one time. Put through wide cutters. Lay out on counter top or table, separate strands, and allow to dry ½ hour before using; or allow to dry thoroughly and store in closed container or in freezer.

To cook, put in a pan of boiling water with small amount of salt and olive oil added. Cook until "al dente" (takes only a few minutes).

Georgia O'Keeffe, American, 1887-
THE GREY HILLS, 1942
oil on canvas, 20 x 30 inches
Gift of Mr. & Mrs. James W. Fessler, 43.37

Sauces for Fettuccini

SALSA ALFREDO

1 cup butter, softened
½ cup heavy cream
1 cup *freshly* grated Parmesan
cheese
1 recipe Pasta Fettuccini
cooked "al dente", drained

Cream butter until light and fluffy. Beat in cream, then Parmesan cheese. Let stand until brought to room temperature. Toss with hot, cooked pasta.

Pass more Parmesan cheese when served.

SALSA DI NOCI

½ cup butter, softened
½ cup grated Parmesan cheese
2 cloves garlic, crushed
1 teaspoon basil
½ teaspoon marjoram
½ cup olive oil
½ cup chopped parsley
¾ cup pine nuts, chopped
(or walnuts)
1 recipe Pasta Fettuccini
cooked "al dente", drained

Blend butter with cheese, garlic, and herbs. Slowly add olive oil. Add parsley and nuts; barely blend. Let stand until brought to room temperature. Toss with hot, cooked pasta.

MUSHROOM MOUSSE WITH SAUCE SUPRÈME

Serves 4 to 6

Duxelles
  1 lb. mushrooms,
    finely chopped
  1 tablespoon chopped shallots
  ½ cup butter
  1 tablespoon lemon juice
Bechamel Sauce
  1 tablespoon butter, melted
  1 tablespoon flour
  ⅓ cup milk
  Salt
  Pepper
  Nutmeg
  3 eggs, separated
Sauce Suprème
  4 tablespoons butter
  4 tablespoons flour
  2 cups chicken stock
  Salt
  Pepper
  Dash of lemon juice
  ¾ cup whipping cream
  2 tablespoons finely julienned
    mushrooms or truffles

Duxelles: Finely chop mushrooms and shallots, squeeze mushrooms in a linen towel. (Squeeze juice into the chicken stock to be used for Sauce Suprème.) Cook the mushrooms with the lemon juice in the butter until the mushrooms are dark and dry, about 20 minutes. Set aside.

Bechamel Sauce: Melt butter in small heavy saucepan; stir in flour and cook, stirring until golden and bubbly. Mix in milk; cook over medium heat until thick. Season with salt, pepper, and nutmeg.

To this Bechamel Sauce add Duxelles. Separate eggs. Stir yolks into the combined sauces, remove from heat, and cool slightly. Fold in the stiffly beaten egg whites. Pour into a heavily buttered 5-cup ring mold. Put in a roasting pan with hot water coming ⅔ up the sides of mold. Bake at 375°F for 25 minutes. Remove from oven and water. Let rest 5 minutes before unmolding.

Sauce Suprème: Melt 4 tablespoons butter in heavy saucepan. Blend in flour and cook until golden, stirring. Gradually stir in the chicken stock, and cook, stirring until thickened. Season with salt, pepper, and dash of lemon juice. Mix in the heavy cream and the mushrooms.

Run a knife blade around edge of mousse to loosen it from the mold. Put a 10-inch platter face down on top of the mold. Invert mousse and pour the Sauce Suprème around and over the top. Serve at once.

Duxelles may be made ahead and frozen. May also be made in and served from a soufflé dish.

Makes a good lunch for four with green salad and French bread.

Brunch, Lunch and Supper

ENTRÉES AND ACCOMPANIMENTS

DILLED SALMON MOUSSE

Serves 8 as Entrée—14 as Appetizer

2 cans salmon: 15½ oz. each
⅓ cup lemon juice
1 cup sour cream
1 cup shredded cheddar cheese
2 tablespoons grated onion
1 teaspoon salt
1 teaspoon dill weed, more, if fresh
2 envelopes gelatin
½ cup water
1 tablespoon vinegar
1 cup whipping cream

Drain salmon; remove bones and skin; flake with a fork. Put salmon in mixing bowl, and add lemon, sour cream, cheese, onion, salt, and dill weed. Heat the gelatin, water, and vinegar together until dissolved. Gradually stir this into salmon mixture. Whip the cream and fold in, just until combined. Turn into a 6-cup fish mold, and refrigerate until firm. Overnight is preferable.

If used as an appetizer, serve with crackers.

Note: Best made with red salmon. Garnish with cucumber slices and tomato wedges or with a cucumber dressing.

George Inness, American, 1825-1894
THE RAINBOW, ca. 1868
oil on canvas, 30¼ x 45¼ inches
Gift of George E. Howe, 44.137

CRAB MEAT AND WILD RICE STRATA

Serves 6 to 8

6 slices bread, crust removed
   and cubed
½ cup minced onions
½ cup diced celery
2 tablespoons butter
½ cup mayonnaise
1 cup cooked wild rice
1 can crab meat: 6½ oz.
2 eggs
1 can mushroom soup: 10¾ oz.
1 cup milk
½ cup shredded sharp cheese

Put one-half of the bread cubes into a greased 1½- to 2-quart casserole. Sauté onions and celery in butter until soft. Combine the onions and celery, mayonnaise, rice, and crab meat. Spread mixture over bread cubes. Cover with remaining bread cubes. Beat eggs, add milk and mushroom soup, and pour over bread. Cover with plastic wrap, and refrigerate overnight. Bake in preheated oven at 350°F for 60 to 65 minutes. Remove from oven and sprinkle with grated cheese. Let stand 10 minutes before serving.

This freezes well.

TROUT AMANDINE

Serves 2

2 trout
⅓ cup butter
½ cup slivered almonds
   Salt
   Pepper
¼ cup lemon juice
   Parsley, chopped

Clean and bone the fish, and place on a serving dish. Cook the butter and almonds until the almonds are lightly browned. Stir often to brown evenly. Season the trout with salt and pepper. Add lemon juice and parsley to the butter and almond mixture. Pour over fish. Cook at 350°F until tender, about 30 to 45 minutes.

Serve with fresh parsley or white grapes.

ARTICHOKE CASSEROLE WITH CRAB OR CHICKEN

Serves 4

1 can artichokes: 14 oz., or
   10 to 12 cooked or
     frozen artichokes
4 hard-boiled eggs, quartered
1½ cups cooked chicken or crab
   meat (preferably frozen)
Sauce
  4 tablespoons butter
  3 tablespoons flour
1½ cups milk
  ¼ cup sherry
  ½ cup shredded Swiss cheese
  2 teaspoons Worcestershire
    sauce
  Salt
  Pepper
  ½ teaspoon curry (optional)

Cut artichokes in half and drain well. Spread artichokes, quartered eggs, and chicken or crab meat in a 2-quart casserole.

Sauce: Blend butter and flour in a pan over low heat. Add milk and combine. Add sherry, cheese, Worcestershire, salt and pepper to taste, and curry, if desired. Pour sauce over casserole, and sprinkle with Parmesan cheese and Chinese noodles, crushed potato chips, or crushed crackers. Bake at 350°F for 30 minutes.

Good brunch dish.

SCALLOPS IN VERMOUTH

Serves 8

3 tablespoons butter
2 to 3 garlic cloves, minced
3 lbs. scallops, fresh or if
   frozen, thawed
½ cup chopped parsley
  Salt
  Pepper
1 cup dry vermouth
¼ cup lemon juice
¼ cup grated coconut (optional)

Melt the butter in a skillet; add garlic and brown lightly. Add scallops, parsley, and seasoning. Sauté 10 minutes, stirring often. Pour into casserole. Mix together lemon juice and vermouth; pour over casserole, and sprinkle with coconut, if desired. Place under broiler until lightly browned, 5 to 10 minutes. Serve immediately.

This may be prepared ahead until the broiling stage, then reheated in the broiler just before serving. Garnish with extra parsley and paprika.

INDIANAPOLIS COLLECTS & COOKS

ORIENTAL ART SOCIETY BRUNCH

Onion Pie
Sliced Ham with Cocktail Buns
Mustard Mold
Poz Noz
Tomartichokes
Lemon Squares

ROQUEFORT AND SHRIMP STUFFED SOLE

Serves 8 to 10

1 cup butter, softened
4 ounces cream cheese, softened
6 ounces shrimp, cut in small pieces
6 ounces Roquefort or Danish bleu cheese
2 tablespoons lemon juice
1 teaspoon chopped parsley
1 teaspoon chopped chives
1 green onion, minced
⅛ teaspoon Tabasco
⅛ teaspoon Worcestershire sauce
8 fillets of sole: 10 oz. each
½ cup butter, melted

Combine the first eleven ingredients. Blend thoroughly. Refrigerate ½ hour. Pat fish dry. Preheat oven to 375°F. Spread ¼ cup chilled filling on darker side of each fillet. Roll fillets, folding in edges to hold filling. Top with remaining filling, if there is any. Place in shallow baking pan, and drizzle with melted butter. Bake at 375°F about 20 minutes, or until sole is white and flaky, but not dry.

A topping of sautéed mushrooms and/or chopped parsley adds a nice touch. These are very generous portions.

Entrées and Accompaniments

TSUNG VASE (ARCHAIC JADE SHAPE)
Lung-ch'uän ware, southern Sung dynasty, A.D. 1127-1279
porcelain, celadon glaze, height 41.2 cm.
Gift of Mr. and Mrs. Eli Lilly, 47.154

FANG-TING (COOKING VESSEL)
Shang dynasty, ca. 1550-1050 B.C.
bronze, height 24.2 cm.
Gift of Eli Lilly, 48.13

COVERED JAR
Ching-te-chen ware, Ming dynasty, Chia-ching period, A.D. 1522-66
porcelain, painted with overglaze polychrome enamels and underglaze blue (wu-ts'ai)
height 45.7 cm.
Gift of Mr. and Mrs. Eli Lilly, 60.88

BOWL
Yung Cheng period, A.D. 1723-1735
famille rose, porcelain, overglaze enamels
Gift of Mr. and Mrs. Eli Lilly, 60.110

SHRIMP-EGGPLANT CASSEROLE

Serves 6

2 medium eggplants, peeled and chopped
1 lb. fresh shrimp, peeled
Butter
2 garlic cloves, minced
½ cup celery, chopped
1 green pepper, chopped
1 onion, chopped
4 cups cooked rice
Dash of red pepper
Dash of black pepper
Cracker crumbs, buttered

Boil eggplants in salt water until tender. Drain and mash. Sauté the shrimp in a small amount of butter until pink. Set aside. Sauté in butter, until wilted, the garlic, celery, green pepper, and onion. Add rice and seasonings. Mix well and place in buttered casserole. Cover with buttered crumbs, and bake for 30 minutes at 350°F.

SHRIMP ÉTOUFFÉE

Serves 3

¾ tablespoon shortening
1 green pepper
1 onion
½ garlic clove
½ stalk celery
1 lb. shrimp
1 tablespoon tomato paste
Salt
Pepper

Coarsely chop pepper, onion, garlic, and celery; and sauté in hot shortening until tender. Reduce heat. Add shrimp and cook slowly until pink. Add tomato paste, season to taste, cover, and simmer 10 minutes, adding a little water if necessary. Serve over white rice.

BEEF SALAMI

Yield: 4 Rolls

5 lbs. lean ground beef
¼ cup curing salt
4 tablespoons dry red wine
2 tablespoons liquid smoke
1½ teaspoons garlic powder
2 tablespoons chili powder
2 teaspoons red pepper flakes
1¼ teaspoons ground cumin
2 tablespoons brown sugar

Mix all ingredients together in large bowl with your hands, making sure salt is evenly distributed. Pack meat down eliminating air pockets; cover; refrigerate for at least 24 hours. Divide into four equal portions, 2½ to 3 inches in diameter, 6- to 8-inches long. Press together, again eliminating air pockets. Roll in cheesecloth; tie ends with string. Bake on rack at 225°F for 4 hours, rolling periodically so they won't flatten. Allow to cool until they can be handled; remove cheesecloth; dry with paper towels. Slice thin to serve.

Can be kept in refrigerator up to three weeks; frozen, six months.

Variations: Omit liquid smoke; use white wine instead or red; use mustard seed, oregano, and sweet basil in place of chili powder, pepper, and cumin; use whole black peppercorns instead of red pepper.

NORTH ITALIAN SAUSAGE

Serves many

20 lbs. coarsely-ground pork (pork butt, untrimmed)
2 ounces total of the following mixed spices: allspice, ground cloves, mace, cinnamon, nutmeg
1 tablespoon dried garlic
1½ ounce black pepper
8 ounces salt
Natural casings, obtained from butcher

Mix together all seasonings. Sprinkle seasonings over cubes of pork before grinding. Soak the casings for a few hours, changing water frequently. Cut off a workable length, insert one end over faucet, and run water through casing. Stuff casings, tying at about 6-inch intervals. Cover with foil and refrigerate overnight. Freeze in packages of 4 to 6. To cook, cover with water; bring to boil, then simmer 20 minutes. Prick casings and simmer an additional 10 minutes. May be browned in skillet.

Serve with catsup, breadsticks, white cheese, hot peppers, green salad. Good in spaghetti or sausage casseroles.

Entrées and Accompaniments

KOREAN FLANK STEAK (Bul-kogi)

Serves 6 to 8

1 flank steak: 2 lbs.
2 tablespoons vinegar
2 tablespoons vegetable oil
2 tablespoons sesame seeds,
    crushed
¼ cup minced green onion
2 tablespoons minced garlic
½ teaspoon minced fresh ginger
2 tablespoons sugar
3 tablespoons soy sauce

Combine all ingredients except soy sauce, and rub on flank steak. Marinate eight to twenty-four hours. Grill meat on a very hot fire until rare. Slice the meat across the grain on the diagonal, and sprinkle with soy sauce.

SPANISH STEAK

Serves 4

1½ lbs. round steak, cut 1¼
    inches thick
1 tablespoon fat or oil
    Dash of black pepper
½ teaspoon salt
1 medium onion, sliced
1 small green pepper, cut into
    strips
1 jar of small pimiento-stuffed
    olives: 2 oz.
1 can tomato soup: 10¾ oz.
½ cup water

Cut meat into serving portions, and brown in hot fat. Place meat in casserole dish, and add black pepper, salt, onion, green pepper, olives (with juice), soup, and water. Cover and bake at 375°F for 1½ hours.

INDIANAPOLIS COLLECTS & COOKS

BEEF VINAIGRETTE

Serves 4 to 6

2 red onions, sliced
¼ cup wine vinegar
¾ cup olive oil
4 tablespoons capers
2 tablespoons chopped parsley
2 teaspoons tarragon
2 teaspoons chopped chervil
2 teaspoons chopped chives
2 teaspoons dry mustard
　Tabasco
2 teaspoons salt
1 teaspoon pepper
4 cups julienne strips of cooked
　roast beef, preferably rare

Combine all ingredients except the beef. Add the beef strips, and marinate three to four hours. Chill well before serving. Serve with a small amount of marinade spooned over the meat.

This may be made several hours before serving. Serve as a hearty salad on lettuce leaves, or it makes a nice second meat course for a buffet.

ONION OR PEPPER STEAK

Serves 4

1 lb. flank steak
3 tablespoons soy sauce
½ teaspoon ginger
4 tablespoons sherry
3 tablespoons corn starch
4 tablespoons oil
2 medium onions, sliced
2 green peppers, seeded and
　cut in strips

Slice steak in thirds lengthwise and trim fat, then slice into ⅛-inch slices across the grain. Mix soy sauce, ginger, sherry, corn starch, and add to steak. Marinate. Put 1 tablespoon oil in large skillet, and heat to smoking. Stir-fry the vegetables keeping them crisp. Remove from skillet. Add remaining oil; reheat and add meat and sauce. Fry lightly; add vegetables to the meat, and cook for another minute or so. Serve with rice.

Minced fresh ginger root about the size of a quarter may be substituted for the ground ginger; fry in oil before adding meat.

Entrées and Accompaniments

HUNGARIAN GOULASH

Serves 4 to 6

3 to 4 lbs. shin of beef,
with bones
3 tablespoons oil
3 large onions, chopped
4 tablespoons sweet Hungarian
paprika
3 to 4 cups chicken or beef
stock, canned or
made from cubes
1 tablespoon mixed herbs
4 medium tomatoes, peeled,
seeded, chopped
3 green or red sweet peppers,
seeded, chopped
Salt
Pepper

Heat oil in 4- to 5-quart heavy casserole or Dutch oven. Add chopped onions and cook slowly until transparent. Add paprika, stir, and cook 3 to 4 minutes over low heat. Skin beef shins and remove visible fat. Detach meat from bone and cube. Add meat, bones, stock, and herbs to onions; stock should cover meat. Bring to boil, lower to simmering point, cover, and cook about 1½ hours, or bake in oven at 350°F. Add green peppers and tomatoes, cover, and cook 40 minutes until meat is tender. Remove meat from casserole. Discard bones. Save gravy in separate container. Refrigerate, skim fat from gravy when cold. Combine meat and gravy, heat and serve.

It can be reheated several times and is better each time. May be frozen.

BAVARIAN POT ROAST

Serves 4 to 6

3 lbs lean, boneless chuck cut
   in 1-inch cubes
¼ cup flour
1½ teaspoons salt
1 teaspoon ground ginger
½ teaspoon ground allspice
½ teaspoon ground cloves
¼ teaspoon ground pepper
3 tablespoons vegetable oil
1 can tomatoes: 8 oz.
¾ cup water
½ cup red wine
¼ cup cider vinegar
2 onions, sliced
2 tablespoons sugar
1 bay leaf

Coat beef with flour mixed with seasonings. Brown well on both sides in vegetable oil. Remove excess oil. Add remaining ingredients, cover, simmer for 1½ to 2 hours, until tender. Thicken liquid for gravy.

   Best made the day ahead, and reheated in a casserole in the oven.

SPICED CORNED BEEF

Serves 8 to 10

4 to 5 lbs. corned beef brisket
   Water to cover
   Whole cloves
½ cup brown sugar
¼ cup fine dry bread crumbs
½ teaspoon dry mustard
   Grated peel and juice of 1
      medium orange
   Grated peel and juice of 1
      lemon
1 cup cider or apple juice

Cover meat with cold water; bring to a boil; turn off heat and skim. Cover and simmer slowly 3 hours. Cool in cooking liquid. Place drained corned beef in baking pan; score fat and stud with cloves. Combine brown sugar, crumbs, mustard, and grated peels. Pat meat with crumb mixture. Place in oven at 350°F. Brown slightly. Baste frequently with a mixture of the orange and lemon juices and cider. Continue baking 45 minutes or until basting mixture caramelizes.

Entrées and Accompaniments

NEAPOLITAN BEEF

Serves 8

¼ cup vegetable oil
3 cloves garlic, crushed
1 cup diced carrots
1½ cups diced celery
⅓ cup finely chopped onion
1½ lbs. ground chuck
1 can tomatoes: 3½ cups
1 can mushrooms: 8 oz.
1 can tomato paste: 6 oz.
½ cup sherry
1 tablespoon salt
½ teaspoon pepper
½ teaspoon oregano
½ teaspoon basil
1 package frozen chopped
   spinach: 10 oz.
1 package small shell
   macaroni: 7 oz.
1 cup grated sharp cheese
½ cup buttered fresh bread
   cubes
  Parmesan cheese

Heat oil in large skillet. Sauté the next four ingredients until golden. Add ground chuck; cook, stirring until lightly browned. Skim off excess fat. Add next eight ingredients. Simmer, uncovered, 1½ hours. Cook spinach and macaroni according to package directions. Drain well, add to sauce. Place in 3-quart baking dish. Top with sharp cheese and bread cubes. Bake uncovered at 350°F for 30 minutes until bubbly and brown. Serve sprinkled with Parmesan.

Sauce may be prepared ahead of time and refrigerated. When ready to serve, reheat sauce, add cooked spinach and macaroni, and bake as directed.

VEAL WITH TARRAGON

Serves 4 to 6

1 tablespoon bacon drippings
1 tablespoon butter
2 lbs. veal, cut in 1-inch cubes
  Salt
  Pepper, freshly ground
2 tablespoons shallots,
  finely chopped
1½ cups chicken broth
1 cup white wine
1 tablespoon dried
  tarragon leaves
1 bay leaf
1 tablespoon butter
1 tablespoon flour
¼ cup heavy cream
  Parsley

Melt bacon drippings and butter in a heavy pot. Add the veal which has been seasoned with salt and pepper. Sauté until veal is browned on all sides. Add shallots and sauté for 3 minutes more. Add chicken broth and wine, which have been heated together with tarragon and bay leaf. Bring to a boil. Reduce heat and simmer, covered, 1½ to 2 hours or until veal is tender. Cream butter and flour, and add cream. Stir into veal and bring to a boil. Serve sprinkled with parsley.

May be served over rice, noodles, or delicate puff pastry patty shells. This is a simple but elegant dish.

VEAL IN LEMON-WINE SAUCE

Serves 4 to 6

1½ lbs. veal scallops, pounded
  thin (see note)
½ cup flour
1 teaspoon salt
6 tablespoons unsalted butter
½ cup dry white wine, heated 15
  minutes over low heat
  Juice of ½ lemon
2 tablespoon minced parsley
  sprigs

Dip scallops in flour and salt mixture. Melt butter in large frying pan. Add veal; turn when edges are white. When both sides are brown, pour in wine and let it bubble a minute or two. Add lemon juice and stir gently. Serve with parsley.

Excellent with Fettuccini Alfredo. Can be kept warm a half hour or so over low heat or in a warm oven before serving.

Note: When pounding veal scallops, push away from you as you pound. Do not tear the meat. If you wet sheets of wax paper between which you put the veal, the meat will not stick. Remove any surrounding membrane before you pound, and pound to ⅛-inch thickness.

Entrées and Accompaniments

TERIYAKI FLANK STEAK

Serves 4

1½ lbs. flank steak
¼ cup soy sauce
¼ cup vinegar
3 tablespoons honey
2 tablespoons salad oil
1½ teaspoons garlic powder
1½ teaspoons ground ginger
2 green onions, finely chopped

Score flank steak on both sides so marinade can soak in. Make marinade of remaining ingredients. Place steak in marinade. Turn often. Let stand 4 to 6 hours . . . longer is better. Barbecue over flaming coals, about 5 minutes on each side for medium rare. Slice meat on diagonal to serve. Slice very thin. Pour heated marinade over meat.

For another taste replace the vinegar with dry sherry, and add sesame seeds.

VEAL MARSALA

Serves 4 to 6

1½ lbs. veal round steak,
    pounded very thin
1 cup sliced celery
1 medium onion, sliced
  Salt
  White pepper
2 packages beef broth
1½ cups water
1 cup Marsala wine
1 cup sliced fresh mushrooms
¼ cup butter
¼ cup grated Parmesan cheese
  Parsley, chopped

Cut meat into serving pieces. Brown in a large skillet in a small amount of oil. Add celery and onion, and brown slightly. Salt and pepper to taste. Sprinkle with beef broth. Add 1½ cups of water. Cover and simmer gently for 30 minutes. Add wine and mushrooms, and simmer 15 minutes. Stir in butter and Parmesan cheese just before serving. Garnish with chopped parsley.

Excellent dish with rice or noodles.

INDIANAPOLIS COLLECTS & COOKS

LAMB STEW

Serves 6 to 8

4 tablespoons shortening
3 lbs. lamb, cut in 1-inch pieces
Salt
Pepper
2 tablespoons flour
2 cups water
1 garlic clove, minced
2 tablespoons tomato paste
3 medium carrots, quartered
5 small onions
5 medium potatoes, quartered
1 teaspoon sugar
6 large mushrooms,
   sliced and sautéed
1 cup peas, cooked (optional)
3 tablespoons sherry

Heat 2 tablespoons shortening in skillet. Season meat with salt and pepper; sprinkle with flour and brown. Add water, garlic, and tomato paste; bring to a boil, stirring constantly. Pour into a 3-quart casserole; cover and bake at 350°F for 30 minutes. Heat remaining 2 tablespoons shortening in skillet. Add carrots, onions, and potatoes. Sprinkle sugar over vegetables, and cook only long enough to glaze them. Pour vegetables into casserole with meat; cover and bake at 350°F for 1 hour. Just before serving stir in mushrooms, peas, and sherry.
Serve at once.

BRUSH AND PAPER HOLDER
18th Century
white nephrite
Gift of Dr. and Mrs. R. Norris Shreve, 71.11.12

STEWED RABBIT OR CHICKEN

Serves 4

1 rabbit, cut in small pieces, or
   1 frying chicken, cut into 8
   pieces: 3 lbs.
½ cup butter
¼ cup olive oil
1 medium onion, chopped
1 cup water
  Salt
  Pepper
  Garlic
  Thyme
  Rosemary
  Bay leaf
  Oregano
½ cup celery, chopped
2 cups tomatoes, Italian

Sauté onion in butter and olive oil. Add rabbit or chicken, and brown about 15 minutes. Add water, spices, celery, and tomatoes. Cover; simmer 2 hours. Serve over polenta or rice.

PORK CHOPS IN WINE

Serves 6

6 pork chops, ¾-inch thick
2 teaspoons prepared mustard
  Salt
  Pepper
¼ teaspoon dry dill
¼ cup brown sugar
6 thin lemon slices
1 cup dry white wine

Trim fat from chops, and grease skillet with it. Brown chops well; drain fat. Spread chops with mustard, seasonings, and brown sugar. Put slice of lemon on each chop. Add wine. Cover and cook 50 to 60 minutes or longer.

POLISH STYLE PORK ROLLS

Serves 4 to 6

6 thin slices pork steak
1 large onion
4 tablespoons butter
¼ cup chopped parsley
1 teaspoon fresh basil or
    ½ teaspoon dried basil
½ lb. sausage
1½ cups dry bread crumbs
  Salt
  Pepper
  Nutmeg
4 tablespoons bacon fat
  or butter
1 cup broth, beer, or water
1 teaspoon butter
2 teaspoons flour
1½ cups sour cream
1 tablespoon paprika
  Salt
  Pepper

First prepare a stuffing. Peel and chop the onion, and sauté it in 4 tablespoons butter until soft. Add the parsley and basil. Mix thoroughly with sausage, bread crumbs, and 1 teaspoon each of salt and pepper. Sprinkle pork slices with a little salt, pepper, and nutmeg. Put a mound of stuffing on each pork slice. Roll up and tie securely. Melt bacon fat or butter in a skillet, and brown the pork rolls on all sides. Reduce the heat and add 1 cup of broth, beer, or water. Cover and simmer for about 45 minutes or until meat is tender. Remove pork rolls to a hot platter. Knead into small pellets 1 teaspoon butter, 2 teaspoons flour, and stir into juices in the pan. Stir until smooth and thickened. Slowly add the sour cream, not letting it boil. Add paprika, and pepper to taste. Pour sauce over pork rolls.
    Serve with buttered noodles.

SAUSAGE LOAF

Serves 6 to 8

1 lb. ground sausage
½ cup corn flakes
¾ cup dried bread crumbs
½ cup water
1 egg, beaten
½ teaspoon salt
½ teaspoon poultry seasoning

Butter a 4-cup ring mold lightly, and sprinkle with ½ cup corn flakes. Combine sausage, dried bread crumbs, water, egg, salt, and poultry seasoning. Press sausage mixture firmly into ring mold. Bake uncovered at 350°F for 1 hour.

Delicious served with scrambled eggs which have been mixed with sautéed mushrooms, minced green pepper, chopped pimiento, and sherry, placed in the center of the sausage ring.

CHICKEN FRICASSEE

Serves 4 to 6

1 frying chicken, cut up: 3½ lbs.
2 garlic cloves, crushed
Salt
Pepper, freshly ground
¼ cup olive oil
½ cup dry white vermouth
⅛ teaspoon saffron
1 large onion, chopped
Water
1 egg yolk
2 tablespoons lemon juice
2 tablespoons parsley, chopped

Combine chicken pieces with garlic, salt, pepper, 2 tablespoons oil, wine, and saffron in a bowl. Turn to cover evenly. Let stand at room temperature for 1 hour. Heat the remaining oil in a heavy casserole. Add onion and cook slowly until tender and golden translucent. Place chicken and marinade on top of onion. Cover and cook slowly for 35 to 40 minutes or until chicken is tender, or bake at 350°F for the same length of time. Stir the mixture two or three times while cooking. If it becomes too dry, add a small amount of water. Combine egg yolk with lemon juice, and stir into the casserole. Reheat, but do not boil. Sprinkle with parsley and serve from the casserole.

Rice is a nice accompaniment.

INDIANAPOLIS COLLECTS & COOKS

HAM LOAF

Serves 6

2 lbs. ham loaf mix, equal parts
   ham, pork, veal
1 cup milk
1 egg, beaten
1 cup coarse bread crumbs
2 onions, chopped
  Salt
  Pepper
1 cup brown sugar
  Pineapple slices

Mix milk, beaten egg, and bread crumbs (any kind). Let mixture stand for 5 or 10 minutes. Add ham loaf mix, onions, and salt and pepper to taste. Put brown sugar in 13 x 8-inch glass baking dish; spread evenly. Form meat loaf and place on sugar. Flatten loaf top carefully. Bake 1¼ hours at 325°F. Put pineapple slices on top of loaf. Bake an additional ½ hour.

Add additional milk for a moister loaf. Good served with a mustard sauce of Poupon mustard mixed with half and half.

ITALIAN SAUSAGE

Serves 3 to 4

1 lb. ground pork
1 teaspoon sage
1 teaspoon salt
1 teaspoon fennel seed
1 teaspoon crushed red pepper

Mix all ingredients together; form into sausage shapes or into patties. Cook in ungreased skillet. Brown on all sides.

This may be added to spaghetti sauce and served with spaghetti. The patties are good with eggs. Also, sauté green pepper and onions in sausage drippings, and serve on sausage or in a sandwich.

PORK TENDERLOIN DELUXE

Serves 6 to 8

2 lbs. pork tenderloin fillets
Butter
1 can asparagus, reserve
    water: 15 oz.
½ lb. mushrooms
2 tablespoons butter
½ cup tomato paste
½ cup cream or half and half
Salt
Pepper

Cut the meat into small steaks, and pound thin. Brown quickly in butter in frying pan. Transfer to a shallow oven dish. Wash mushrooms and sauté lightly in butter. Spread the mushrooms and asparagus over the meat, arranging on each piece of meat. Melt 2 tablespoons butter in pan, and add ¼ cup asparagus water, tomato paste, and cream. Season with salt and pepper. Pour the sauce over the meat and vegetables, and heat at 400°F for 15 minutes.

Chicken breasts, veal, or thin pork chops (boned) may be substituted for pork tenderloin.

ASPARAGUS HAM BAKE

Serves 6

1½ cups packaged cornbread
    stuffing or
    herb-seasoned stuffing
2 cups diced cooked ham
2 cups fresh or frozen
    asparagus, cut, cooked,
    and drained; or 1 can cut
    asparagus: 16 oz.
1 tablespoon butter, melted
Cheese Sauce
  1 can cream of celery soup:
     10¾ oz.
  1 cup milk
  ¼ cup chopped onion
  ⅛ teaspoon marjoram
  $\frac{1}{16}$ teaspoon rosemary
  ½ cup shredded sharp cheese

Place ⅓ of the dry stuffing over the bottom of a 1½-quart greased casserole; top with half the ham, asparagus, and cheese sauce. Repeat layer. Mix the remaining ⅓ stuffing with melted butter, and sprinkle over top of casserole. Bake for 35 minutes at 350°F.

When serving, casserole may be topped with buttered asparagus.

INDIANAPOLIS COLLECTS & COOKS

SWEET AND SOUR PORK

Serves 4

1 lb. lean pork, fat-trimmed and cubed
Flour
1 tablespoon fat
1 medium onion, thinly sliced
2 tablespoons brown sugar
1 tablespoon soy sauce
2 tablespoons vinegar
1½ cups chicken stock or 2 chicken bouillon cubes, dissolved
½ cup green pepper, cut in squares
½ cup pineapple chunks or more to taste
1 small jar pimientos: 2 oz.
⅓ to ½ cup sliced mushrooms
Cornstarch for thickening, if needed

Dust pork in flour, and brown in fat. Add next five ingredients, and simmer 30 minutes. (If cooked pork is used, simply add rest of ingredients immediately.) Add remainder of ingredients. Cover and simmer 20 minutes. If sauce needs thickening, mix a little cornstarch in a small dish with water to make a smooth paste.

Leftover pork roast makes this a quick and easy dish.

RETREAT AT THE FOOT OF HUI MOUNTAIN
Wang Meng, ca. 1308-1385 A.D.
hand scroll; ink on paper
Gift of Mr. and Mrs. Eli Lilly, 60.50

SPANISH CHICKEN (Gallina Guisada)

Serves 6

3 garlic cloves, minced
½ medium onion, minced
1 teaspoon pepper
3 tablespoon lemon juice
¼ cup vegetable oil
6 whole chicken breasts, split
3 fresh tomatoes,
    skinned and mashed
  Salt

Blend garlic, onion, and black pepper with lemon juice. Sauté chicken in oil until brown. Add the lemon juice mixture. Cook for 15 minutes, then add the tomatoes which have been mashed. Cover and simmer for about 50 minutes. Add salt to taste.
   Serve with Saffron Rice.

HERB CHICKEN CASSEROLE

Serves 6

3 large chicken breasts, halved
  Salt
  Pepper
¼ cup butter
1 can cream of chicken soup:
    10¾ oz.
¾ cup sauterne
1 can water chestnuts, drained
    and sliced: 5 oz.
1 can broiled, sliced
    mushrooms, drained: 3 oz.
2 tablespoons green pepper,
    chopped
¼ teaspoon crushed thyme

Lightly season chicken with salt and pepper; brown slowly in butter in skillet. Arrange browned chicken skin side up in a 11½ x 7½ x 1½-inch baking dish. Add soup to drippings in skillet; slowly add sauterne while stirring until smooth. Add remaining ingredients; heat to boiling. Pour sauce over chicken. Bake covered at 350°F for 25 minutes. Uncover; continue baking 25 minutes or until tender.

INDIANAPOLIS COLLECTS & COOKS

BASQUE CHICKEN

Serves 5 to 6

1 tablespoon butter
3 tablespoons olive oil
4 whole chicken breasts, split
½ lb. fresh mushrooms, sliced
1 medium onion, chopped
2 cans tomato paste: 6 oz. each
½ cup very dry sherry
10 small white onions, canned, if
    fresh unavailable
4 sprigs parsley
1 teaspoon salt
⅛ teaspoon pepper
½ cup small stuffed olives
2 medium green peppers,
    cut in strips
3 medium tomatoes,
    cut in wedges

Heat butter and oil in Dutch oven, and brown chicken on all sides. Remove. Sauté mushrooms and onions in the same pan until lightly browned. Stir in tomato paste, sherry, small onions, and parsley. Return chicken to pan; sprinkle with salt and pepper; simmer covered until tender, about 30 minutes. Baste occasionally with sauce. After 15 minutes of cooking add olives. Place chicken on large platter, and keep warm. Simmer sauce uncovered for 5 minutes. Heat 1 tablespoon olive oil in skillet, and sauté green pepper about 2 minutes. Add tomatoes and cook until hot. *Do not overcook.* Arrange tomatoes, peppers, and small onions on platter with chicken. Serve with Saffron Rice and sauce.

ROLLED CHICKEN WASHINGTON

Serves 6 to 7

½ cup finely chopped
  mushrooms or 1 can,
  drained and chopped: 3 oz.
2 tablespoons butter
2 tablespoons flour
½ cup light cream
¼ teaspoon salt
  Dash of cayenne pepper
1¼ cups shredded sharp
  cheddar cheese
6 or 7 boned whole chicken
  breasts, skinned
  Flour
2 eggs, slightly beaten
¾ cup fine dry bread crumbs

Cook mushrooms in butter about 5 minutes. Blend in flour; stir in cream. Add salt and cayenne; cook and stir until mixture becomes very thick. Stir in cheese; cook over very low heat, stirring constantly until cheese is melted. Turn mixture into a pie plate. Cover and chill thoroughly 1 hour. Cut the firm cheese mixture into 6 or 7 equal portions. Shape into short sticks.

To make cutlets, place each piece of chicken, boned side up, between two pieces of wax paper, overlapping meat where chicken breast is split. Working out from the center, pound with mallet to form cutlets not quite ¼-inch thick. Peel off wax paper. Sprinkle meat with salt. Place a cheese stick on each chicken breast. Tuck in the sides, and roll chicken as for jelly roll. Press to seal well. Dust the chicken rolls with flour, dip in slightly beaten egg, and roll in fine dry bread crumbs. Cover and chill chicken rolls at least 1 hour. They can be prepared ahead and chilled overnight. Fry rolls in deep, hot fat at 375°F for 5 minutes or until crisp and golden. Drain on paper towel. Place rolls in shallow baking dish, and bake at 325°F for 30 to 45 minutes.

BAKED CHICKEN WITH WINE

Serves 6

6 whole chicken breasts, split
Salt
Pepper
1 can mushroom soup: 10¾ oz.
¼ cup dry sherry
Paprika

Place chicken breasts in shallow baking dish, and add salt and pepper. Blend mushroom soup with wine until smooth. Pour sauce over chicken, and sprinkle generously with paprika. Bake uncovered 1¾ hours at 300°F, until chicken is tender and well browned on top.

Slivered almonds and Parmesan cheese may be added as topping.

CHICKEN WITH GARLIC AND LEMON

Serves 4

8 chicken thighs
2 tablespoons olive oil
Juice of 1½ lemons
½ lemon, sliced thin
4 garlic cloves, mashed
2 tablespoons
fresh parsley, minced
Salt
White pepper
1 cup chicken broth
2 tablespoons dry vermouth
2 tablespoons butter
2 tablespoons flour

Brown chicken thighs in oil. Add lemon juice, sliced lemon, garlic, parsley, salt, pepper, chicken broth, and vermouth. Simmer 30 minutes. Melt butter in a small pan, add flour and stir. Add this roux to chicken mixture, and simmer 10 minutes. Serve with rice.

CHICKEN WITH FORTY CLOVES OF GARLIC

Serves 6

2 broiler-fryers: 3½ lbs. each or 8 leg quarters
2 to 3 large heads of garlic*
⅔ cup olive oil
4 ribs celery, sliced thin on bias
8 to 10 sprigs parsley
1 rounded tablespoon salt
White pepper, freshly ground
Dash of nutmeg

*One head of garlic will yield about 20 cloves, and if you are apprehensive about this amount of garlic, relax. The long cooking subdues it and turns it into a delicate, delicious butter.

Drop the garlic into a saucepan of rapidly boiling water for 10 seconds or so. Drain and run under cold water. Trim tops and bottoms, and slip off outside skins. Set aside. Pour oil into heavy casserole with a lid. Turn chicken pieces over in oil so they are well coated. Place one half the chicken in the casserole. Sprinkle with one half the celery, parsley, garlic, and salt. Season with pepper and a dash of nutmeg. Place remaining chicken in casserole, and repeat. Cover with heavy-duty foil, sealing edge tightly, and then add cover. Bake in preheated oven at 375°F for 1½ hours. Do not open during baking period. Serve from casserole.

BODHISATTVA MAHASTHAMAPRAPTA
Chinese, Sui dynasty, A.D. 581-618
gilt-bronze, height 31.7 cm.
Gift of Mr. and Mrs. Eli Lilly, 60.47

OVEN CHICKEN SALAD

Serves 6

2 cups cubed cooked chicken
1 can French fried onions:
   3½ oz.
1 cup sliced celery
½ cup chopped salted cashews
3 tablespoons lemon juice
½ cup chopped green pepper
¼ cup chopped pimiento
¼ teaspoon sweet basil
¼ teaspoon salt
1 cup mayonnaise
½ cup milk
   Paprika

Mix one-half can of onions with all ingredients except paprika. Place in 1½-quart casserole. Bake uncovered for 30 minutes at 350°F. Top with remaining onions and paprika.
Bake 5 minutes. Serve.

BARBECUED CHICKEN WITH HONEY GLAZE

Serves 4 to 6

2 frying chickens, cut into
   pieces
1 can tomato sauce: 8 oz.
½ cup orange juice
¼ cup vinegar
½ cup olive oil
1½ teaspoons crushed oregano
1 teaspoon salt
6 peppercorns, crushed
1 garlic clove, minced
¼ cup honey
½ teaspoon dry mustard

Combine tomato sauce, orange juice, vinegar, olive oil, oregano, salt, crushed peppercorns, and minced garlic. Pour over chicken pieces. These may be parboiled for less cooking time. Marinate for 2 hours at room temperature or overnight in refrigerator. Barbecue the chicken on a grill, brushing with marinade and turning occasionally. Combine the honey and dry mustard, and brush over chicken before serving.

Entrées and Accompaniments

CHICKEN IN THE OLD STYLE

Serves 6

1 fryer, cut up: 3 to 4 lbs.
 Salt
 Pepper
4 tablespoons olive oil
1 large lime, juice plus
  grated rind
2 ripe tomatoes, seeded,
  chopped
3 tablespoons raisins
¼ teaspoon oregano
1 onion, chopped
1 garlic clove, chopped
1 medium pineapple or 2 cups
  crushed, canned pineapple
3 teaspoons light rum

Rub lime juice into chicken pieces. Add salt and pepper. Let stand 1 hour. Heat oil; fry chicken until brown. Transfer to casserole with juices. Cover and cook over low heat until barely tender. Add tomatoes, raisins, rind, oregano, onion, and garlic. Cover and cook gently for 10 minutes. Simmer pineapple in saucepan to one-half volume. Add rum and pour over chicken. Serve.

CHICKEN CHAUFROID

Serves 6 to 8

6 to 8 chicken breasts, skinned,
  boned, and flattened
Topping
 ½ cup mayonnaise
 6 ounces cream cheese
 1 tablespoon dill weed
 3 tablespoon lemon juice
 1 teaspoon lemon rind, grated
 ½ teaspoon salt
 ¼ cup slivered almonds
Garnish
 1 avocado, sliced
 ½ cup mandarin oranges
  Lettuce

Poach chicken breasts 20 minutes. Chill. Cream mayonnaise, cream cheese, dill, lemon juice, rind, and salt to form a smooth paste. Spread topping on chilled chicken breasts. Top with slivered almonds. Garnish with avocado slices and mandarin oranges. Serve on lettuce leaves.

INDIANAPOLIS COLLECTS & COOKS

MUSTARD MOLD

Serves 8

4 eggs
1 envelope gelatin
¼ cup water
1½ tablespoons dry mustard
¾ cup sugar
¼ teaspoon salt
½ cup cider vinegar
½ pint whipping cream, whipped

Beat the eggs in the top of a double boiler using a wooden spoon. Add the gelatin which has been softened in the ¼ cup of water, mustard, sugar, and salt. Stir and add the vinegar. Place over boiling water, and stir constantly in one direction until thickened mixture coats a spoon. Cool 30 minutes. Fold in whipped cream, and put in a lightly oiled 6-cup mold.
Chill overnight.
   This is especially good with Canadian bacon at a brunch, but also nice with ham, turkey, or roast beef on a buffet.

YORKSHIRE PUDDING

Serves 8 to 10

2 cups flour, sifted
1 teaspoon salt
2 cups milk, cold
4 eggs, cold
½ cup beef drippings from rib
   roast, sizzling hot

Sift together flour and salt. Gradually add milk, beating until smooth. Add eggs, one at a time, beating until smooth. Cover and chill at least 2 hours. Beat cold batter until smooth. Pour *hot* beef drippings into a 9 x 13-inch pan. Pour batter into pan; bake at 425°F for 25 to 30 minutes or until pudding is puffy, crisp, and brown. Cut into squares and serve immediately.
   Serve with standing rib roast or any good beef roast. The secret to Yorkshire Pudding is to have the batter cold and the beef drippings sizzling hot!

Entrées and Accompaniments

TURKEY WITH ORANGE RICE

Serves 12 to 14

1 turkey: 12 lbs.
3 cups water
1 teaspoon salt
1 teaspoon leaf rosemary
3 chicken bouillon cubes or
   3 teaspoons instant chicken
   bouillon
1½ cups brown rice
6 slices bacon
½ cup green onions, sliced
2 tablespoons butter
1 can water chestnuts, drained,
   sliced: 8 oz.
¾ cup frozen orange juice
   concentrate, thawed,
   undiluted: 6 oz.
¼ cup sherry

In medium saucepan combine water, salt, rosemary, and bouillon; and bring to boil. Add uncooked brown rice. Cover; simmer 30 minutes or until liquid is absorbed. Fry bacon crisp; crumble. Add bacon, green onion, butter, and water chestnuts to rice; and mix well. Add 3 tablespoons orange juice concentrate. Reserve remainder for basting. Stuff turkey with rice mixture. Place in large brown bag, close bag, and staple. Bake at 325°F for 4 to 4½ hours. Remove bag from turkey. Combine orange juice and sherry, and brush on turkey. Bake for an additional 15 to 20 minutes.

PINEAPPLE DRESSING

Serves 10 to 12

1 can crushed unsweetened
   pineapple, drained: 20 oz.
2 cups sugar
1 cup butter, melted
4 eggs
8 slices, cubed day-old bread,
   crust removed
Bread crusts, crumbed

Combine all ingredients, except bread crust crumbs. Top with bread crust crumbs. Bake in a greased 1½-quart casserole, uncovered, at 350°F for ½ to ¾ hour.

Serve warm or chilled as accompaniment to pork and ham. Good with sausage and eggs for brunch. Leftovers can be dessert the next day.

CHICKEN PIE

Serves 8

2 cups cooked chicken, cubed very fine
4 cups Fricassee Sauce
3 egg yolks, beaten well
1 cup fresh mushrooms, sliced
¼ teaspoon salt
¼ teaspoon pepper
¾ cup chopped almonds, toasted
3 egg whites, stiffly beaten
1 unbaked pastry shell
Fricassee Sauce
½ cup chicken fat
½ cup flour
3 cups chicken broth, heated
Salt
Pepper

Fold beaten egg yolks into 2 cups of Fricassee Sauce. (The remaining sauce may be heated and served over the pie slices.) Add chicken, mushrooms, and seasonings to the egg yolk and Fricassee Sauce mixture. Add almonds and fold in the stiffly beaten egg whites. Pour into an unbaked pie shell, and bake at 350°F for 40 minutes.

To make Fricassee Sauce, melt fat in a skillet and add flour. Stir and cook for 5 minutes. Add hot broth and cook for 10 minutes. Add salt and pepper to taste.

SPICED FRUIT WITH PORT

Serves 6 to 8

1 can pitted Bing cherries: 8 oz.
1 can peach slices: 16 oz.
1 can pear halves: 16 oz.
4 slices lemon
2 cinnamon sticks
3 whole cloves
3 whole allspice
½ teaspoon powdered ginger
½ cup port wine

Drain syrups from the fruit into a saucepan. Set aside the fruits in a bowl. Add the lemon and spices to the syrups, and boil for 20 minutes. Add the port and pour the syrup over the fruits. Return the fruits and sauce to the pan, and let the flavors blend for several hours. Before serving, heat the compote until warm.

A good recipe to use when oven space is not available.

SAUCES

TARRAGON SHRIMP SAUCE

Yield: 1½ Cups

1 cup mayonnaise
3 hard-cooked eggs, finely
   chopped
2 tablespoons chopped capers
2 tablespoons minced parsley
2 tablespoons minced green onion
1 teaspoon Dijon mustard
1 tablespoon tarragon vinegar
1 tablespoon lemon juice
1 clove garlic, minced
1 teaspoon horseradish
1 teaspoon chopped fresh
   tarragon or ½
   teaspoon dried tarragon

Combine all ingredients. Pour sauce over cooked shrimp.
   Serve with your favorite cracker.

HOT SWEET AND SOUR SAUCE FOR AVOCADOS

Serves 8

6 tablespoons beef consommé
3 tablespoons red wine vinegar
3 tablespoons chili sauce
3 tablespoons red currant jelly
4 avocados, peeled and halved

Combine consommé, vinegar, chili sauce, and currant jelly. Heat in a double boiler until very hot. Pour over peeled and seeded avocado halves, and serve immediately.

SPICED MUSTARD SAUCE

Yield: 1 Cup

1 cup sour cream
2 tablespoons Dijon mustard
1 tablespoon soy sauce
1 tablespoon Worcestershire
   sauce
1 teaspoon finely grated onion
1 garlic clove, minced
  Salt
  Pepper

Combine all ingredients. Refrigerate in covered jar until needed. Will keep indefinitely.
   This sauce is nice served with beef fondue, on sandwiches, over vegetables, or on cold meat.

INDIANAPOLIS COLLECTS & COOKS

DOROTHY'S FISH SAUCE

Yield: ¾ Cup

¼ cup butter
3 tablespoons soy sauce
1 tablespoon Worcestershire
   sauce
¼ cup dry white wine
1 tablespoon lemon juice
   Fillets of whitefish, trout,
   or sole
   Parsley, chopped

Combine ingredients and heat to melt butter and blend. Spoon over the fillets 3 hours before cooking. Refrigerate. Brush fish with sauce before and during broiling. Garnish with parsley and serve.

HONEY ALMOND SAUCE FOR VEGETABLES

Yield: ¾ Cup

½ cup butter
½ cup slivered almonds
2 tablespoons honey
¼ teaspoon lemon juice
   Salt
   Pepper
   Parsley, chopped

Melt butter and add almonds. Cook until almonds are brown. Add honey, lemon juice; and season with salt and pepper to taste. Pour over cooked vegetables, such as butternut squash, green beans, carrots, or asparagus. Top with chopped parsley.

OLIVE ANCHOVY SAUCE (Tapenade)

Serves 8 to 10

24 to 30 pitted Greek or
   Italian olives
3 or 4 garlic cloves
1½ tablespoons capers
¼ cup olive oil, or more
14 to 16 anchovy fillets
1 can tuna, oil packed: 4 oz.
   Olive oil to make paste
1 or 2 tablespoons cognac
1 tablespoon Dijon mustard

In a blender or food processor place the pitted olives, garlic, capers, and ¼ cup olive oil. Blend until smooth, adding more olive oil if necessary to make a paste. Remove to a bowl. In same blender container combine the anchovy fillets, tuna, and enough olive oil to make a paste. Blend the two pastes together. Add the cognac and mustard. Blend all together to make a thick purée. Taste for seasoning. It may need more cognac, some black pepper, hot pepper, a touch of thyme, or savory.

This is a delicious and versatile sauce. It will keep a long time in your refrigerator, ready for instant use as a sauce for hard-boiled eggs, fish, or raw green vegetables.

Sauces

VEGETABLES

TOMATO ONION CHEESE CASSEROLE

Serves 6 to 8

3 cups thinly sliced onions
4 large ripe tomatoes, peeled
    and sliced, or 3 cups
    canned
1 teaspoon salt
¼ teaspoon pepper
½ teaspoon dried basil
4 slices sharp cheddar cheese,
    halved
½ cup seasoned bread crumbs
3 tablespoons butter

Preheat oven to 350°F. Lightly grease a 1½-quart casserole. In 1 inch of boiling water in a medium saucepan, cook onions, covered, for 10 minutes. Layer in the casserole half of tomatoes, onions, salt, pepper, basil, and cheese. Repeat. Toss bread crumbs with butter, and sprinkle over the top of the casserole. Bake, uncovered, at 350°F for 30 to 35 minutes, or until tomatoes are tender.

RAISIN SAUCED BEETS

Serves 4 to 6

1 can sliced beets: 1 lb.
½ cup seedless raisins
1 tablespoon cornstarch
¼ cup sugar
3 tablespoons lemon juice
2 tablespoons butter
½ teaspoon salt
$^1/_{16}$ teaspoon pepper

Drain liquid from beets into saucepan. Add raisins and simmer until raisins are plumped. Combine cornstarch and sugar. Add to mixture in pan along with lemon juice, butter, salt, and pepper. Cook, stirring constantly, until mixture comes to boil and is thickened. Stir in beets and simmer until beets are hot.

INDIANAPOLIS COLLECTS & COOKS

BROCCOLI CASSEROLE

Serves 6

3 cups cooked and chopped
   broccoli
3 ounces cream cheese
1½ cups milk
1 tablespoon lemon juice
1 tablespoon chopped parsley
2 eggs
1 teaspoon chopped basil
½ teaspoon salt
   Pepper

Cook and drain broccoli. Blend cream cheese and milk; add to broccoli. Add remaining ingredients, and pour into a greased baking dish. Bake slowly at 325° F for 1 hour.

BRIGHT GREEN BROCCOLI

Serves 8

1 bunch fresh broccoli: 1½ to 2
   lbs.
½ cup peanut oil
1½ teaspoons minced garlic
1 teaspoon salt
¼ teaspoon white pepper

Cut off broccoli florets, and separate to bite size. Peel hard stalk with a sharp knife. Cut stalk and stems into 1½-inch slender pieces. Rinse well in running water, and drain on paper towels. Stir-fry the garlic in oil over high heat until it begins to brown. Add broccoli. Cook, stirring constantly, for 4 minutes. Reduce heat and cook covered for 2 minutes. Uncover. Increase heat and cook 2 more minutes. Serve immediately.

   This broccoli dish is beautiful, crisp, and delicious.

PEPPERS ROQUEFORT

Serves 8

4 plump perfect green peppers
1 cup Roquefort cheese,
   crumbled
1 cup bread crumbs, packed
⅔ cup mayonnaise
⅔ cup milk
   Salt

Halve peppers lengthwise. Remove stem, seeds, and membrane. Cover with water and parboil for 5 minutes. Crumble cheese and blend with remaining ingredients. Fill peppers with mixture, and place in shallow 8 x 11½-inch baking dish. Peppers should be packed tightly together. Add small amount of water, enough to cover bottom of baking dish. Bake uncovered at 350°F for 25 minutes, until lightly brown.

Easy to prepare and delicious.

RICE CAKES

Serves 4

1 cup cooked rice
4 scallions, chopped
2 tablespoons parsley
¼ cup flour
2 eggs
   Salt
   Pepper
2 tablespoons butter

Mix together all ingredients except the butter. Form into four flattened patties. Heat butter to sizzling, but not brown, and sauté the rice patties.

Rice cakes may be formed ahead, refrigerated, and sautéed at serving time.

SAFFRON RICE

Serves 6 to 8

1 tablespoon butter
1½ cups uncooked brown rice
1 can chicken broth: 10½ oz.
1 can water
1 teaspoon salt
1 teaspoon onion salt
   Pinch of saffron

Combine ingredients and bake at 350°F for 1½ hours, uncovered, or 45 minutes, covered.

PRINT AND DRAWING SOCIETY
FALL DINNER MEETING

Woodland Farms Dilled Carrots
Sweet and Sour Pork with Rice
Bright Green Broccoli
Praline Cheesecake

SAVORY SWEET PEPPERS

Serves 8 to 10

3 red peppers: 1 lb.
3 green peppers: 1 lb.
2 tablespoons vegetable oil
1 tablespoon wine vinegar
½ teaspoon salt
½ teaspoon oregano
⅛ teaspoon freshly ground pepper

Wash peppers. Cut in half lengthwise, and remove ribs and pulp. Cut each half in fourths lengthwise, or eighths if peppers are large. Heat oil in skillet. Add peppers and cook over medium heat, stirring occasionally until peppers are just tender, about 15 minutes. Gently stir in vinegar, salt, oregano, and pepper.

Delicious served with grilled meat or cold chicken as a patio supper.

HERBED NEW POTATOES

Serves 6

1½ lbs. new potatoes
4 tablespoons butter
1 tablespoon lemon juice
Salt
Pepper
1 tablespoon chives
2 heads fresh dill, chopped
3 tablespoons snipped parsley

Scrub potatoes. Pare strip around the center. Cook in boiling salted water for 25 minutes. Drain and return to pan. Combine butter, lemon, and herbs; stir into potatoes to coat well.

Can be kept in oven on *low* heat for limited time. Fresh parsley makes flavorful garnish.

Vegetables

Jean François Raffaëlli, French, 1845-1924
TO YOUR HEALTH, 1894
color etching
Bequest of Delavan Smith, 25.49

Georges Braque, French, 1881-1963
STILL LIFE III, 1921
color lithograph
Gift of the Gamboliers, 32.153

Jacques François Amand, French, 1730-1789
ROMAN TOWN
sanguine
James B. Sweetser Fund, 57.106

Charles Demuth, American, 1883-1935
THREE PEARS AND A PEACH
watercolor
Alliance—Better Than New Fund, 73.11

SKILLET POTATO SALAD

Serves 6

1 tablespoon butter
1 cup chopped onions
½ cup mayonnaise
⅓ cup cider vinegar
1¾ teaspoons salt
¼ teaspoon fresh ground
  pepper
4 medium potatoes, cooked,
  peeled, and sliced
1 tablespoon parsley
¼ cup green pepper, chopped
  (optional)
1 tablespoon bacon, cooked,
  crumbled

In large skillet cook onions in butter over medium heat for 2 or 3 minutes. Stir in next 5 ingredients. Add potatoes, and green pepper, if used. Heat through about 2 minutes, stirring constantly. Garnish with parsley and bacon. *Do not allow to boil.*

GREEN RICE

Serves 4

2 cups cooked rice
1 egg, beaten
1 cup milk
½ cup finely chopped parsley
1 clove garlic, finely chopped
1 small onion, minced
½ cup grated sharp cheese
1 green pepper, finely chopped
  Salt
2 tablespoons olive oil

Mix all ingredients together except olive oil. Pour olive oil into a 1½-quart baking dish and add rice mixture. Bake for 30 minutes at 350°F.

CABBAGE AND EGGPLANT IN CHEESE SAUCE

Serves 8 to 10

1 cabbage, shredded: 2 lbs.
¼ cup chopped onion
4 tablespoons butter
1 eggplant, peeled and diced: 1 lb.
8 tablespoons butter
¼ cup flour
1 lb. sharp cheddar cheese, grated
2 cups beer
¼ cup Worcestershire sauce
1 teaspoon salt
1 teaspoon dry mustard
Tabasco
White pepper
1 cup fresh bread crumbs
½ teaspoon paprika

Cook cabbage in boiling, salted water for 5 minutes. Drain well and put in bowl. Sauté onion in butter until soft. Add eggplant and cook until soft. Add to cabbage. In saucepan melt 8 tablespoons butter, add flour, cook, and stir on low heat for 3 minutes. Stir in cheddar cheese, ¼ cup at a time; and remove pan from heat. Stir in beer and cook over moderate heat until it is hot but not boiling. Add rest of the seasonings, and cook sauce for 5 minutes. Stir in cabbage mixture and transfer to casserole. Sprinkle with fresh bread crumbs and paprika. Bake at 350°F for 15 minutes.

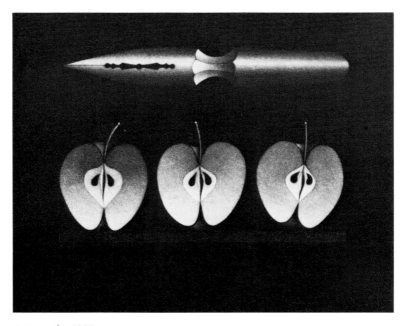

Mario Avati, French, 1921-
LA PLUME DU SERGENT
mezzotint
Martha Delzell Memorial Fund, 72.131.6

CARROTS OR PARSNIPS AND CABBAGE

Serves 6 to 8

6 medium carrots or parsnips
1 medium head cabbage
2 medium onions
4 stalks celery
2 tablespoons milk
1½ teaspoons sugar
2 tablespoons butter
1 egg (optional)
4 ounces cream cheese
  Dash of garlic salt
  Dash of dill
  Salt
  Pepper
½ cup bread crumbs
½ cup grated sharp cheese
  Butter

Boil together the carrots (or parsnips), cabbage, onion, and celery until tender, about 5 to 8 minutes. Mash with milk, sugar, butter, (egg), cream cheese, and seasonings. Place in casserole, cover with bread crumbs and grated cheese, and dot with butter. Bake at 350°F for 30 minutes.

SMOTHERED CABBAGE WEDGES

Serves 8

1 medium cabbage, cut into
  8 wedges
½ cup finely chopped green
  pepper
¼ cup finely chopped onions
4 tablespoons butter
¼ cup flour
½ teaspoon salt
⅛ teaspoon pepper
2 cups milk
½ cup mayonnaise
¾ cup grated cheddar cheese:
  3 oz.
3 tablespoons chili sauce

Cook cabbage in salted water until tender, about 12 minutes. Drain well. Place wedges in 13 x 9 x 2-inch baking dish. Cook green pepper and onion in butter until tender. Blend in flour, salt, and pepper. Add milk all at once; cook and stir until mixture thickens. Pour over cabbage wedges. Bake uncovered at 375°F for 20 minutes. Combine mayonnaise, cheese, and chili sauce. Spoon over wedges. Bake 5 minutes more.

INDIANAPOLIS COLLECTS & COOKS

BAKED CAULIFLOWER

Serves 6

1 head cauliflower
1½ cups canned tomatoes, drained
½ cup chopped onion
½ teaspoon oregano
½ teaspoon salt
⅛ teaspoon pepper
¾ cup grated sharp cheddar cheese
¾ cup coarse cracker crumbs

Break cauliflower into florets, and cook in water until just tender, about 20 minutes. In a greased 2-quart casserole combine tomatoes, onion, oregano, salt, and pepper. Cover with cauliflower. Mix cheese and crumbs. Sprinkle over cauliflower. Bake at 400°F for 20 minutes.

This is a nice change from the usual cauliflower with cream sauce.

CELERY AMANDINE

Serves 8

1 cup blanched almonds, sliced and browned
½ teaspoon finely chopped garlic
½ cup butter, divided
4 cups celery, sliced diagonally in ½-inch pieces
1 teaspoon salt
Dash of pepper
3 teaspoons finely chopped green onions
2 tablespoons dry white wine

Cook almonds and garlic in ¼ cup butter, stirring to brown uniformly. Set aside. Melt ¼ cup butter in large skillet. Add celery, salt, and pepper. Cover and cook over low heat 10 minutes until tender, but still a bit crisp. Add green onions; cover and cook 2 minutes. Add wine to almonds, and heat about 1 minute. Turn the hot celery into a serving dish. Spoon the almonds over the top.

Vegetables

BAKED EGGPLANT CREOLE

Serves 4

1 large eggplant
⅓ stick butter
3 tablespoons flour
2 cups tomatoes, canned
    or fresh
2 green onions, chopped
½ green pepper, chopped
¼ teaspoon red pepper
1 teaspoon salt
2 tablespoons brown sugar
1 bay leaf
½ cup cracker or bread crumbs
    Butter

Pare eggplant, cut into small cubes, and boil in salted water for ten minutes. Drain and put in buttered baking dish. Melt butter in skillet; add flour and blend. Add tomatoes, onion, green pepper, and spices. Cook 5 minutes. Pour over eggplant, cover with crumbs, and dot generously with butter. Bake at 350°F for 30 minutes.

BAKED EGGPLANT

Serves 4 to 6

1 large eggplant
5 cups soft bread crumbs
⅔ cup celery, chopped
2 medium tomatoes, peeled
    and chopped
1 onion, chopped
2 beaten egg yolks
2 tablespoons melted butter
1½ teaspoons salt
    Pepper

Cut eggplant in half lengthwise. Remove inside from shell, and cook in boiling salted water 20 minutes. Drain well and mash. Add remaining ingredients and mix thoroughly. Place in skins that have been buttered, then place in pan with small amount of water. Bake 375°F for 1¼ hours.

Grated cheese may be added fifteen minutes before shells are done.

MUSHROOM AND CHEESE ZUCCHINI

Serves 6

3 medium zucchini, 6 to 8
  inches long
1 cup chopped fresh
  mushrooms
2 tablespoons butter
2 tablespoons flour
¼ teaspoon oregano
¼ teaspoon lemon pepper
  seasoning
½ teaspoon salt
1 cup shredded provolone or
  Swiss cheese
2 tablespoons sour cream

Cook whole zucchini 8 to 10 minutes. Cut in half lengthwise. Remove and reserve pulp leaving ¼-inch shell. (A melon baller makes removing the pulp easier.) Drain shells. Sauté mushrooms in butter until cooked. Stir in flour, oregano, and seasonings. Remove from heat and stir in cheese, sour cream, and zucchini pulp. Fill shells and broil 5 minutes.

MUSHROOMS AND CREAM

Serves 4

1 lb. fresh mushrooms
⅓ cup soft butter
1 tablespoon minced parsley
1 tablespoon minced onion
1 tablespoon Dijon mustard
1 teaspoon salt
  Pinch of cayenne
  Pinch of nutmeg
1½ tablespoons flour
1 cup heavy cream or less to
  make it less soupy

Clean mushrooms and cut off stems. Cream together the butter, parsley, onion, mustard, salt, cayenne, nutmeg, and flour. Place mushrooms in a one-quart casserole. Dot with the butter mixture, and pour on the cream. Bake at 375°F for 1 hour, uncovered. Stir once or twice during baking.

Nice to serve with steak or hamburgers from the grill.

Vegetables

WILD RICE WITH MUSHROOMS

Serves 8 to 10

1 cup wild rice
½ lb. mushrooms, sliced
2 tablespoons butter
4 slices bacon, chopped fine
1 or 2 celery stalks, coarsely
    chopped
1 medium onion, coarsely
    chopped
1 large green pepper, coarsely
    chopped
½ cup tomato juice
5 tablespoons olive oil
1 teaspoon salt

Soak wild rice in cold water for 30 minutes. Rinse well and cook in 3 cups water until tender, about 30 minutes; drain well. Meanwhile sauté mushrooms in butter. In another pan fry chopped bacon until crisp; add celery, onion, and green pepper. Sauté vegetables 1 to 3 minutes; vegetables should not be limp. Combine rice and sautéed vegetables with tomato juice, olive oil, and salt in a 2-quart casserole. Bake at 350°F for 30 minutes.

May be made ahead and refrigerated. Chopped pimiento may be added just before baking for color.

SPINACH WITH FRESH CREAM

Serves 4 to 6

3 lbs. fresh spinach or
    4 packages frozen chopped:
    10 oz. each
  Salt
4 tablespoons butter
½ cup whipping cream
  Pinch of sugar
  Dash of nutmeg (optional)

Wash spinach well. Cook in large saucepan with small amount of boiling water. When it has boiled down (this will happen fast as spinach needs little cooking), add salt. Drain and when cool, squeeze as dry as possible; then chop fine. In a saucepan melt butter and stir in spinach. Heat until warm and add pepper, sugar, nutmeg, and more salt, if desired. Heat cream just to boiling point and stir in gradually. Keep warm in a double boiler.

MUSHROOMS AND ZUCCHINI IN WINE SAUCE

Serves 6

1½ lbs. small zucchini, sliced lengthwise
3 tablespoons butter
1 small onion, finely chopped
3 tablespoons flour
1 cup milk
1 chicken bouillon cube
⅓ cup white wine
4 ounces fresh mushrooms, sliced
2 tablespoons chopped parsley
½ teaspoon Worcestershire sauce
Salt
Pepper
½ cup grated American cheese
Paprika

Prepare zucchini and cook in boiling salted water until barely tender. Drain well and place in greased shallow baking dish. Melt butter and add onion and cook, blending in flour, milk, and chicken bouillon cube. Cook until thick. Add wine, mushrooms, parsley, Worcestershire sauce, salt, and pepper. Pour sauce over zucchini. Sprinkle with cheese and paprika. Bake at 375°F for 35 minutes or until bubbly.

SPINACH AND RICE CASSEROLE

Serves 6

1 cup instant rice
2 packages frozen chopped spinach: 10 oz. each
2 medium onions
4 tablespoons butter
1½ cups Cheez Whiz

Prepare rice as directed on package. Cook and drain spinach. Chop onions and sauté in butter. Mix rice, spinach, onions, and 1 cup of cheese. Place in casserole and top with remaining cheese. Bake at 350°F for 30 minutes.

Vegetables

BAKED SPINACH AND ARTICHOKES

Serves 8

2 packages frozen chopped spinach: 10 oz. each
½ cup butter
8 ounces cream cheese
1 can artichokes (hearts or bottoms): 16 oz.
4 tablespoons lemon juice

Cook and drain spinach. Melt butter and mix with softened cream cheese. Cut artichoke hearts in half (or use canned bottoms or pieces). Line bottom of baking dish with artichokes. Mix spinach, lemon juice, and cheese; and pour over artichokes. Bake at 350°F for 30 to 40 minutes.

RICE RING MARIA

Serves 8

2 cups long grain rice
2 teaspoons salt
1 lb. fresh asparagus
1 cup heavy cream or half and half
½ cup butter
¼ cup freshly grated Parmesan cheese
3½ ounces Fontina cheese
3½ ounces Gruyère cheese

Cook the rice in 4 cups water with 2 teaspoons salt for 15 minutes. Prepare the asparagus. While the asparagus is cooking, warm the cream in a double boiler or heavy saucepan over low heat. Into it put one-half the butter, one-half the Parmesan, and all the Fontina and all the Gruyère. Stir frequently. Stir the remaining butter and Parmesan into the cooked rice, using a fork. Turn the rice into a 6-cup ring mold. Cover with foil and place in oven at 400°F for 5 minutes. Then unmold on a round platter. Surround the ring with the freshly cooked asparagus, and fill the center with the cheese sauce which should be very hot and smooth. Serve additional cheese sauce on the side.

Do not substitute cheeses. This is excellent served with lamb or fresh fish.

SPICED SWEET POTATOES

Serves 6 to 8

3 lbs. sweet potatoes or
40-ounce can
½ cup brown sugar
3 tablespoons butter
½ teaspoon cinnamon
½ teaspoon nutmeg
¼ teaspoon salt
2 eggs
½ cup coffee cream

Boil sweet potatoes until soft. Peel and rice. (If using canned potatoes, drain before ricing.) Stir in sugar, butter, cinnamon, nutmeg, and salt. Beat eggs lightly with cream. Add to above. Turn mixture into casserole; bake at 400°F for 15 to 20 minutes.

To add extra flavor, stir in grated orange zest and ¼ cup brandy or Grand Marnier. Sprinkle top with granulated sugar and/or almonds before baking.

SUMMER SQUASH CASSEROLE

Serves 6 to 8

3 to 4 lbs. summer squash,
sliced
½ cup dry herb dressing mix,
divided
1 large carrot, grated
8 tablespoons butter
1 medium onion, diced
1 cup sour cream
1 can cream of chicken soup:
10¾ oz.

Parboil squash for 2 to 3 minutes; drain well. Grease a 2-quart casserole, and sprinkle bottom with ¼ cup dry herb dressing mix. Combine all of the other ingredients. Pour into casserole and sprinkle top with the other ¼ cup dressing mix. Bake at 350°F for 45 minutes.

This may be prepared the day before and baked the day of use.

SQUASH PARMESAN

Serves 8

12 small summer squash or
zucchini, sliced: 2 quarts
1 medium onion, sliced
4 tablespoons butter
⅔ cup sour cream
½ to ¾ cup Parmesan cheese,
grated
½ teaspoon salt

Cook sliced squash until tender in small amount of water. Sauté onion in butter until soft, and set aside. Drain and mash squash. Add sour cream and reserved onions. Mix and put into a casserole. Sprinkle with grated cheese, and brown under the broiler.

Vegetables

CHEDDAR ZUCCHINI BAKE

Serves 8 to 10

6 cups zucchini, thinly sliced, unpared
2 egg yolks, slightly beaten
1 cup sour cream
2 tablespoons flour
2 egg whites, stiffly beaten
1½ cups shredded cheddar cheese
6 slices bacon, fried crisp and crumbled
1 tablespoon melted butter
¼ cup dry bread crumbs

Simmer zucchini until tender; drain and sprinkle with salt. Combine egg yolks, sour cream, flour, and fold in egg whites. Place half of the zucchini in a 12 x 7½ x 2-inch baking dish; top with half of the egg mixture, half of the cheese, and all of the bacon. Repeat layers of zucchini, egg mixture, and cheese. Sprinkle butter and crumbs on top. Bake at 350°F for 20 to 25 minutes.

ZUCCHINI CASSEROLE

Serves 8

8 to 10 small to medium zucchini
½ cup butter
¾ cup grated cheddar cheese
¼ cup grated Swiss cheese
1 cup sour cream
½ teaspoon salt
⅛ teaspoon paprika
¼ cup chopped chives or green onion tops
1 cup bread crumbs
Grated Parmesan cheese.

Wash zucchini and boil whole until *just tender,* about 10 minutes. Cut off ends and cut in half lengthwise.Drain. Arrange in a buttered casserole. Melt butter and mix in cheeses and sour cream. Add salt, paprika, and chives. Pour mixture over zucchini, and sprinkle bread crumbs on top. Dot with butter and sprinkle with Parmesan cheese. Bake at 350°F until cheese bubbles, approximately 30 to 45 minutes.

Rembrandt Harmensz Van Rijn, Dutch, 1606-1669
THE PANCAKE WOMAN, 1635
etching
Bequest of Delavan Smith, 25.21

SWEET AND SOUR BEAN CASSEROLE

Serves 12

8 slices bacon
4 large onions
1½ cups brown sugar
1 tablespoon dry mustard
½ teaspoon garlic powder
1 teaspoon salt
½ cup vinegar
2 cans dried lima beans:
    15 oz. each
1 can green lima beans: 15 oz.
1 can dark red kidney beans:
    15 oz.
1 can garbanzo beans: 15 oz.
2 cans pork and beans, do not
    drain: 15 oz. each

Dice and fry bacon crisp with thinly sliced onions. Cook brown sugar, dry mustard, garlic powder, salt, and vinegar for 20 minutes. Drain all cans of beans *except* the pork and beans. Mix together and bake at 325°F for 1½ hours.

Can be refrigerated or frozen and reheated.

GRITS CASSEROLE

Serves 8

1 cup grits
1 roll garlic cheese, or sharp,
    nippy cheese: 6 oz.
½ cup butter
2 eggs, beaten
¼ cup milk
½ teaspoon salt
½ teaspoon pepper, black or red
1 cup grated cheddar cheese
    Paprika

Cook grits in 3 cups water according to directions on package. Add the garlic cheese, cut in chunks, and butter to the hot grits, and stir until melted. Add the beaten eggs, milk, salt, and pepper. Pour into a greased casserole, and bake 45 minutes at 350°F. Remove from oven. Sprinkle with grated cheddar cheese and paprika, and bake 10 minutes more.

Delicious served with ham or barbecued chicken.

GREEN VEGETABLE CASSEROLE

Serves 8 to 10

3 green peppers, sliced thin
1 package frozen baby lima
    beans
1 package frozen small green
    peas
1 package frozen French style
    green beans
1 cup whipping cream, whipped
1 cup mayonnaise
    Parmesan cheese

Cook green peppers in water until tender; drain. Cook vegetables as directed; drain well. Combine vegetables and mayonnaise, and fold in whipped cream. Put in buttered casserole, and sprinkle with Parmesan cheese. Bake until brown at 350°F.

INDIANAPOLIS COLLECTS & COOKS

Giovanni Battista Tiepolo, Italian, 1693-1770
TWO STUDIES FOR MOSES
pen and ink
Gift of Mrs. William H. Thompson, 47.15

TOMATOES WITH BACON AND OLIVES

Serves 6

3 large tomatoes
Salt
Pepper
Garlic or garlic salt
Basil
Sugar
4 green olives, chopped
2 slices of bacon, shredded

Cut tomatoes into halves. Season with sugar, salt, pepper, garlic, and basil. Place olives and bacon on top of each half. Broil and watch closely, or bake at 425°F for 10 to 15 minutes until tops are slightly brown.

These may be prepared ahead of serving, refrigerated and re-warmed or served cold. Very good with grilled meats.

Olives and bacon may be replaced with herbs to taste—for instance, oregano, dill weed—and/or onions, bread crumbs, Parmesan, Worcestershire, brown sugar.

Use your imagination!

ASPARAGUS WITH SAUCE

Serves 8

2 tablespoons butter
3 tablespoons flour
1 teaspoon salt
⅛ teaspoon pepper
1 cup chicken broth
½ cup cream or half and half
1 egg yolk, slightly beaten
1 teaspoon lemon juice
1 can mushrooms, drained: 2 oz.
1½ lbs. asparagus, cooked, or
　　2 cans asparagus spears,
　　drained: 15 oz.
½ cup bread crumbs, browned
　　and buttered

Melt butter. Blend in flour and seasonings. Add broth and cream. Cook, stirring constantly until thick and smooth. Add small amount of hot mixture to egg yolk, and blend. Return to sauce and cook, stirring constantly, for 3 minutes. Stir in lemon juice and mushrooms. Place asparagus in a shallow casserole. Top with sauce and cover with crumbs. Bake at 350°F for 15 minutes or until heated through.

May be made ahead and heated before serving.

INDIANAPOLIS COLLECTS & COOKS

HORTICULTURAL SOCIETY PICNIC
AT THE HORTICULTURAL STUDY CENTER

Savory Beef Stuffed Cherry Tomatoes
Garden Relish Tray
Dilled Salmon Mousse
Watercress Mushroom Salad
Beef Salami
Herb Cheese Bread
Pralines

YUGOSLAVIAN VEGETABLE CASSEROLE

Serves 12 or more

1 potato, diced
1 medium zucchini, unpeeled and diced
1 medium eggplant, unpeeled and diced
2 green peppers, diced
2 small carrots, quartered lengthwise and cut in 1-inch strips
1 Bermuda onion, coarsely chopped
½ cup shelled fresh peas
2 tablespoons chopped parsley
⅓ cup olive oil
1 tablespoon salt
1 teaspoon Tabasco
1 teaspoon freshly ground pepper
4 large tomatoes, sliced
⅓ cup raw rice
½ cup olive oil
2 tablespoons white wine vinegar
1¾ cups grated cheddar cheese

Combine potato, zucchini, eggplant, green peppers, carrots, onion, peas, and parsley with ⅓ cup olive oil, salt, Tabasco, and pepper. Line an oiled 9 x 11-inch baking dish with half the vegetable mixture. Layer with half the tomato slices, sprinkle with rice, add remaining vegetables, and top with remaining tomato slices. Mix remaining ½ cup olive oil with vinegar, and pour over casserole. Bake, covered, at 350°F for 1¾ hours. Sprinkle with cheese and place under broiler until cheese is melted.

Can be made two days ahead. Freezes well after baking.

Vegetables

Paul Gauguin, French, 1848-1903
LANDSCAPE NEAR ARLES, 1888
oil on canvas, 36 x 28½ inches
Gift in memory of William Ray Adams, 44.10

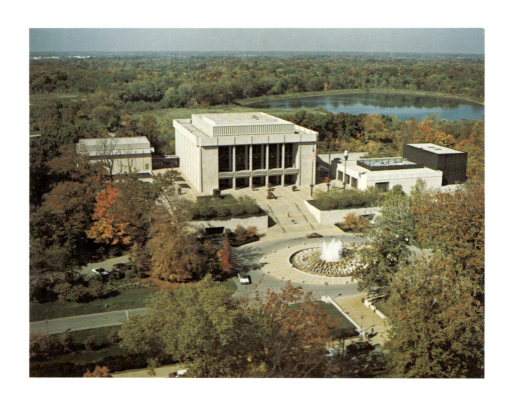

AERIAL VIEW, INDIANAPOLIS MUSEUM OF ART
KRANNERT, CLOWES AND SHOWALTER PAVILIONS
Ambrose Richardson, A.I.A., Principal architect

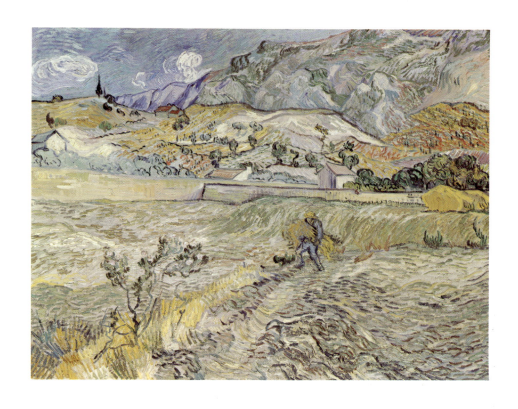

Vincent van Gogh, French, born Holland, 1853-1890
LANDSCAPE AT SAINT-REMY (THE PLOUGHED FIELD), October 1889
oil on canvas, 29 x 36¼ inches
Gift in memory of Daniel W. and Elizabeth C. Marmon, 44.74

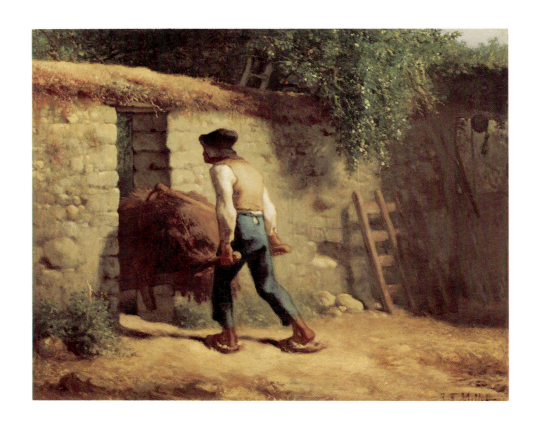

Jean François Millet, French, 1814-1875
PEASANT WITH A WHEELBARROW, 1848-1852
oil on canvas, 14⅞ x 17⅞ inches
James E. Roberts Fund, and Gift of the Alumni Association
of the John Herron Art School, 49.48

SALADS AND SALAD DRESSINGS

CURRIED CHICKEN SALAD

Serves 16

6 whole chicken breasts,
  cooked and cooled:
  6 to 7 cups
1 cup mayonnaise
½ cup milk
1½ tablespoons curry powder
1 teaspoon salt
1 teaspoon pepper
2 cups long grain rice, cooked
  in chicken broth and cooled
1½ cups raw zucchini, *see note*
1 bottle creamy French
  dressing: 8 oz.
1 cup chopped green pepper
1 cup chopped red onion
¼ cup chopped fresh parsley

Cut chicken into large cubes. Mix mayonnaise, milk, curry powder, salt, and pepper together; and toss lightly with cubed chicken. Toss cooled rice with zucchini, and mix them with the French dressing. Combine with chicken and toss lightly so chicken holds shape. At serving time add green pepper, onion, and parsley; toss lightly.

Serve on lettuce. Garnish with toasted slivered almonds and cherry tomatoes.

Note: Peel zucchini very lightly, leaving traces of green color showing. Chop same size as pepper and onion.

ARTICHOKE RICE SALAD

Serves 6 to 8

1 package chicken-flavored
  rice-vermicelli mixture:
  8 oz.
4 scallions, sliced
½ green pepper, chopped
12 medium stuffed olives, sliced
2 jars marinated artichoke
  hearts, halved: 6 oz. each
⅓ cup mayonnaise
¾ teaspoon curry powder

Cook the rice mixture according to directions. Be careful not to overcook as rice will be too soft for salad. Cool. Combine in serving bowl with the scallions, pepper, and olives. Drain the artichoke hearts and reserve the marinade. Cut the hearts in half, and add to the rice mixture. Combine the marinade with the curry powder and mayonnaise using a fork or wire whisk. Toss the dressing with the rice mixture, and chill until serving time.

This is a great picnic salad, and it also freezes well.

INDIANAPOLIS COLLECTS & COOKS

COBB SALAD

Serves 6 to 8

½ head lettuce
½ bunch watercress
1 small bunch chicory
½ head romaine
2 medium tomatoes, peeled
    Juice of 1 or 2 lemons
2 cups diced cooked chicken
    (white meat only)
8 strips bacon, cooked crisp
1 avocado
3 hard cooked eggs, chopped
2 tablespoons chopped chives
½ cup finely grated
    Roquefort cheese

Cut the salad greens into fine pieces, and place in a large salad bowl. Dice the tomatoes and arrange in a row across salad. Arrange the diced chicken over greens. Crumble bacon over salad. Cut avocado into small pieces; dip in lemon juice to prevent discoloration, and arrange around the edge. Decorate salad by sprinkling with the chopped eggs, chives, and Roquefort cheese. Just before serving, mix salad thoroughly with French dressing or a dressing of your choice.

This is a very hearty salad and can precede a light meal or serve as a main dish for a buffet or a ladies' luncheon.

CHUTNEY CHICKEN SALAD

Serves 50

25 cups cooked chicken breasts
12 hard-boiled eggs
 4 cups water chestnuts
 2 cups chopped scallions
 4 cups chopped celery
 4 cups chopped green peppers
 6 cups mayonnaise
2½ cups chutney
 8 tablespoons white wine
    vinegar
10 teaspoons curry powder
16 tablespoons light cream
 8 teaspoons salt

Day before serving, cook chicken; remove from bone, and cut into bite-sized pieces (about one-half chicken breast per serving). Cook eggs and chop. Coarsely chop water chestnuts. Chop celery, green pepper, and scallions. Cover each tightly and refrigerate. Combine mayonnaise, chutney, vinegar, curry powder, cream, and salt, and refrigerate. Before serving, mix well with chicken, eggs, water chestnuts, celery, green pepper, and scallions. Cover and refrigerate ½ hour or a little more.

Salads and Salad Dressings

TOMARTICHOKES

Serves 6

6 big red tomatoes
Salt
Pepper
Dill weed
6 artichoke hearts, canned
½ cup mayonnaise
½ cup sour cream
1 teaspoon lemon juice
2 tablespoons fresh parsley, chopped
1 tablespoon green onion, chopped
¼ teaspoon Krazy Mixed-Up Salt
¼ teaspoon seasoned salt

Drop the tomatoes into boiling water for a few seconds so the skins will slip off easily. Cut off the tops; scoop out the seeds and juice. Season them inside and out with salt, pepper, and dill. Put an artichoke heart into each tomato. Make a dressing with the mayonnaise and sour cream. Add the lemon juice, parsley, green onion, and salts. Refrigerate tomatoes and dressing. Just before serving arrange on lettuce, and spoon the dressing over each.

MOLDED ASPARAGUS SALAD

Serves 10

1 can asparagus soup, undiluted: 10½ oz.
1 package lime gelatin: 3 oz.
8 ounces cream cheese
½ cup cold water
½ cup mayonnaise
1 teaspoon lemon juice
1 cup chopped celery
1 tablespoon chopped chives
½ cup chopped green pepper
½ cup chopped pecans

Heat soup to boiling. Remove from heat; add lime gelatin and stir until dissolved. Add cheese cut in small pieces and mix well. Add water, mayonnaise, and lemon juice; beat until well blended. Stir in remaining ingredients. Pour into mold and chill until firm.

INDIANAPOLIS COLLECTS & COOKS

BROCCOLI SALAD

Serves 8 to 10

1 large bunch fresh broccoli or
    2 packages frozen:
    10 oz. each
1 cup chopped celery
¼ cup chopped onion
2 hard-boiled eggs, chopped
1 jar pimiento-stuffed olives: 2 oz.
1 cup mayonnaise or ½ cup
    plain yoghurt and ½ cup
    mayonnaise
1 teaspoon lemon juice
  Salt

Steam broccoli in a little water until tender crisp, or cook frozen broccoli until just barely done. Drain and cut fresh broccoli into 1-inch pieces. Mix cut broccoli with remaining ingredients, stirring thoroughly. Cover and refrigerate overnight.

Serve in lettuce-lined bowl, and garnish with tomato wedges. Good with grilled meats in the summer, but delicious with anything.

GARDEN RELISH TRAY (Gardiniera)

Serves 6

½ small head cauliflower, cut in
    florets and sliced
    lengthwise
2 carrots, peeled, cut in
    2-inch strips
2 stalks celery, cut in 1-inch
    pieces: 1 cup
1 green pepper, cut in
    2-inch strips
1 jar pimiento or roasted
    peppers, drained, cut in
    strips: 4 oz.
1 jar pitted green olives,
    drained: 3 oz.
¾ cup wine vinegar
½ cup olive oil
2 tablespoons sugar
1 teaspoon salt
½ teaspoon dried
    oregano leaves
¼ teaspoon pepper

In a large skillet combine ingredients with ¼ cup water and bring to boil. Stir a few times; reduce heat. Simmer, covered, 5 minutes (no longer). Cool. Refrigerate at least 24 hours. Drain well. Serve.

This will keep a week or longer in the refrigerator. Here are fresh vegetables ready to serve on an instant's notice.

Salads and Salad Dressings

FRESH MUSHROOM SALAD

Serves 4 to 6

½ lb. mushrooms
½ cup vegetable oil
¼ cup wine vinegar
¼ cup chopped parsley
 1 teaspoon salt
 1 teaspoon sugar
½ teaspoon garlic powder
¼ teaspoon pepper
 1 tomato, cut in wedges
 1 small sweet onion, sliced

Rinse, pat dry, and slice mushrooms; place in serving bowl. Combine all the other ingredients except tomato wedges and onion slices. Mix well. Pour over mushrooms and toss well to coat. Add tomato and onion, toss. Cover and refrigerate 1 hour before serving.

WATERCRESS-MUSHROOM SALAD

Serves 8

3 bunches watercress, trimmed
   and dry
½ to 1 lb. mushrooms, sliced
¼ cup wine vinegar
⅓ cup olive oil
⅓ cup vegetable oil
 1 small clove garlic, minced
½ teaspoon dry mustard
 1 teaspoon salt
½ teaspoon sugar
¼ teaspoon pepper

Combine watercress and mushrooms. Combine remaining ingredients and blend well. Just before serving, add dressing to coat lightly. Toss.

PEA AND PEANUT SALAD

Serves 6

5 or 6 green onions, finely
　chopped (use some of
　the tops)
2 celery ribs, finely sliced
1 cup Spanish peanuts
¼ cup mayonnaise
2 tablespoons Italian
　salad dressing
1 package frozen green peas,
　thawed: 10 oz.

Combine all ingredients except peas. Just before serving, add peas. Serve on lettuce leaves.

HOT BAKED POTATO SALAD

Serves 8

8 medium potatoes, cooked
　and cooled
¾ lb. American or pimiento
　cheese, diced
1 cup mayonnaise
⅓ cup onion, chopped
½ teaspoon salt
½ teaspoon pepper
⅓ cup bacon, cut in pieces,
　fried limp
¼ cup stuffed olives, sliced

Peel and dice potatoes. Combine potatoes, cheese, mayonnaise, and onion. Reserve some cheese for topping. Add salt and pepper. Place in 7 x 11-inch baking dish. Top with reserved cheese, bacon, and olives. Bake for 1 hour at 325°F.

Flavor is better if made ahead and reheated at serving time.

Salads and Salad Dressings

MOLDED SPINACH SALAD

Serves 10

1 package lemon gelatin: 6 oz.
1 cup hot water
½ cup cold water
2 teaspoons lemon juice
½ cup mayonnaise
1 cup chopped fresh spinach
1 cup cottage cheese, drained
½ cup diced celery
1 teaspoon grated onion

Dissolve gelatin in hot water. Stir in cold water, lemon juice, and mayonnaise. Add remaining ingredients; pour into 5-cup mold, and chill.

SWEET AND SOUR SPINACH SALAD

Serves 6 to 8

3 slices bacon
½ cup sugar
¼ cup water
¼ cup red wine vinegar
1 egg, beaten
½ teaspoon salt
1 bag spinach: 10 oz.
1 small red onion, sliced

Fry bacon until crisp. Remove from pan and crumble. To bacon fat add sugar, water, vinegar, egg, and salt. Stir constantly, cooking for 1 minute. Strain and cool to room temperature. Do *not* refrigerate. Add to washed and dried spinach just before serving. Top with onion rings.

HEARTY CHEESE SALAD

Serves 8 to 10

2 lbs. unprocessed Gruyère or
   Swiss cheese, shredded
1 cup stuffed olives, sliced
2 cups green onions, finely
   chopped
Dressing
1 cup olive oil
¼ cup red wine vinegar
4 teaspoons Dijon mustard
1 teaspoon salt
   Pepper, freshly ground

Combine the cheese, olives, and green onions. Toss with the following dressing, and serve on salad greens.
Dressing: Combine all ingredients and mix well.
   Serve as entrée with crusty French bread and a hearty red wine.

INDIANAPOLIS COLLECTS & COOKS   139

HERBED TOMATOES

Serves 6

6 small tomatoes, peeled
⅔ cup vegetable oil
¼ cup tarragon vinegar
½ teaspoon thyme
½ teaspoon marjoram
1 teaspoon salt
¼ teaspoon pepper
⅓ cup chopped parsley
⅓ cup chopped chives
2 tablespoons chopped
 fresh dill

Combine the vegetable oil, vinegar, thyme, marjoram, salt, and pepper. Mix well and marinate the tomatoes for 2 to 3 hours. Before serving, roll in parsley, chives, and dill. Serve on lettuce.

Save the marinade. It makes a good salad dressing for another time.

ZUCCHINI SALAD

Serves 12

⅔ cup cider vinegar
2 tablespoons red wine vinegar
⅓ cup vegetable oil
1 teaspoon salt
½ teaspoon pepper
½ cup diced onion
½ cup chopped green pepper
½ cup diced celery
8 medium zucchini, sliced thin
1 jar diced pimiento: 2 oz.

Combine and marinate 5 hours or longer. Serve on a lettuce leaf.

One teaspoonful of sugar can be added to marinade for more mellow taste.

Salads and Salad Dressings

PICKLED BEET GELATIN SALAD

Serves 6 to 8

1 jar pickled beets, finely diced, drained, reserve juice: 1 lb.
1 package lemon gelatin: 3 oz.
¾ teaspoon salt
Dash of white pepper
1 cup boiling water
1 teaspoon horseradish
2 teaspoons grated onion
¾ cup finely diced celery

Dissolve gelatin and salt in boiling water. Add beet juice plus enough water to make ¾ cup liquid. Add seasonings and chill until almost set. Fold in beets and celery. Chill until firm.

Garnish with mixture of sour cream and mayonnaise. Serve on crisp lettuce.

TOMATO SURPRISE

Serves 12

3 packages raspberry gelatin: 3 oz. each
1½ cups boiling water
2 cans stewed tomatoes: 20 oz. each
¼ teaspoon Tabasco
1 tablespoon horseradish
1 carton whipped cream cheese with chives: 4 oz.
1½ tablespoons mayonnaise
2 avocados
Chives (optional)

Dissolve raspberry gelatin in boiling water. Stir in stewed tomatoes, Tabasco, and horseradish. Pour into 2-quart ring mold or 12 individual molds; chill until firm. Mix whipped cream cheese and mayonnaise together. Refrigerate. To serve cut the avocados into slices and place around the unmolded salad. Top with cream cheese-mayonnaise mixture and chives.

INDIANAPOLIS COLLECTS & COOKS   141

STRAWBERRY MOLD

Serves 12

2 packages frozen sliced
   strawberries: 1 lb. each
2 packages strawberry gelatin:
   3 oz. each
8 ounces cream cheese
½ cup sour cream
½ teaspoon salt
¾ cup walnuts or pecans,
   chopped

Pineapple Dressing
  1 cup pineapple juice
¾ cup sugar
  1 tablespoon flour
   Juice of 1 lemon
  2 eggs, well beaten
  1 cup whipped cream

Thaw strawberries and drain very well. Add enough water to juice to make 3 cups. Heat to boiling. Pour over gelatin; stir until dissolved, and chill until partially thickened. Fold in strawberries. Pour half into a 9 x 5-inch loaf pan. Chill until firm. Beat cheese until smooth. Add sour cream and salt. Mix well. Stir in nuts. Spoon over jellied layer, spreading gently. Chill until firm. Add remaining strawberry mixture, and again chill until firm. Serve with Pineapple Dressing.

Pineapple Dressing: Combine all ingredients except the whipped cream. Cook until thick. Cool. To one cup of whipped cream add ¾ cup of the pineapple mixture.

Recipe may be doubled to fill an 11-inch ring mold. Serves 28 to 30.

Salads and Salad Dressings

BLUEBERRY SALAD

Serves 12

½ pint cream
1 cup sugar
1 envelope gelatin
¼ cup water
1 teaspoon vanilla
½ pint sour cream
1 package raspberry gelatin: 3 oz.
1 can blueberries and juice: 15 oz.

Heat cream and sugar together. Add gelatin dissolved in the ¼ cup water, vanilla, and sour cream. Pour into mold and let stand 45 minutes. Dissolve raspberry gelatin in boiling water, and add can of blueberries and juice. Pour over cream mixture. Refrigerate.

If using fresh blueberries, add 1½ cups water with 1½ pints blueberries, some mashed. Garnish with a touch of sour cream.

ARABIAN ORANGES

Serves 6 to 8

6 large navel oranges
½ cup slivered almonds,
    blanched
¾ cup chopped pitted dates
⅔ cup orange juice
⅓ cup brandy or kirsch

Peel oranges and slice thin. Add remaining ingredients and chill well.

Good for a brunch.
Delicious and different.

ROQUEFORT MOUSSE SALAD

Serves 6

1 envelope gelatin
¼ cup lemon juice
1 cup boiling water
¼ lb. Roquefort cheese
1 cup grated cucumber
4 tablespoons minced parsley
2 tablespoons minced pimiento
1 tablespoon minced capers
1 teaspoon grated onion
  Salt
  Pepper
1 cup whipping cream, whipped

Soften gelatin in lemon juice, and dissolve in hot water. Thoroughly mash cheese and combine with grated-minced ingredients. Salt and pepper to taste. Stir into the dissolved gelatin. Cool and chill the mixture just until it begins to gel, then fold in whipped cream. Spread the mousse in a 6-cup ring mold, and chill for 4 hours until completely firm. Unmold on a chilled serving plate.

Fill the center with your favorite seafood salad, and garnish with parsley dusted with paprika, or fill with cherry tomatoes.

INDIANAPOLIS COLLECTS & COOKS

GERMAN POTATO SALAD DRESSING FOR ENDIVE

Serves 6 to 8

½ cup vinegar
½ cup water
¾ cup sugar
3 or 4 slices of bacon, diced
1 tablespoon flour
3 or 4 potatoes, boiled
    and diced
1 onion, chopped
  Endive

Mix together the vinegar, water, and sugar; and stir until sugar dissolves. Set aside. Fry bacon until crisp. Add flour to the bacon and grease, and stir. Add the vinegar, water, and sugar mixture. Let come to a good boil. Add the diced potatoes and onions. Pour hot sauce over endive when ready to serve.

This is a hearty summer salad.

VINAIGRETTE À L'ITALIENNE DRESSING

Yield: 1 Cup

1 teaspoon Dijon mustard
1 egg yolk of a 2-minute,
    soft-boiled egg
1 large garlic clove, mashed
  Salt
  Pepper
3 anchovy fillets
2 tablespoons wine vinegar
6 tablespoons olive oil
1 tablespoon grated Parmesan
    cheese

Mix mustard with yolk, garlic, salt, pepper, and anchovies. Mash with fork until smooth. Add vinegar and slowly whisk in olive oil. Add Parmesan cheese.

May be served with spinach or other salad greens. Decorate with finely-sliced red onions.

POPPY SEED DRESSING

Yield: 3 Cups

1½ cups sugar
2 teaspoons dry mustard
2 teaspoons salt
⅔ cup vinegar
3 tablespoons onion juice
2 cups vegetable oil
3 tablespoons poppy seed

Mix sugar, mustard, salt, and vinegar. Add onion juice and stir thoroughly. Add oil slowly, beating constantly until thickened. Add poppy seed and beat a few minutes. Store in the refrigerator.

Good for fruit or vegetable salads.

Salads and Salad Dressings

TABBOULEH

Serves 4 to 6

½ cup fine bulgur wheat
   (crushed wheat)
3 medium tomatoes,
   finely chopped
1 cup finely chopped parsley
1 cup finely chopped onions
⅓ cup lemon juice
2 teaspoons salt
⅓ cup olive oil
2 tablespoons fresh mint, finely
   cut, or 1 tablespoon dried
   mint, crumbled
   Romaine lettuce

Place wheat in bowl, and pour over it enough water to cover. Soak for 10 minutes, then drain in sieve or colander lined with double thickness of dampened cheesecloth. Wrap wheat in cheesecloth, and squeeze until completely dry. Place wheat in deep bowl. Add tomatoes, parsley, onions, lemon juice, and salt. Toss gently but thoroughly with fork. Just before serving, stir in olive oil and mint. Taste for seasoning. Spoon onto romaine lettuce leaves.

CELERY SEED FRUIT SALAD DRESSING

Yield: 1¼ Cups

1 teaspoon celery seed
1 teaspoon salt
1 teaspoon dry mustard
1 teaspoon paprika
½ teaspoon grated onion
½ cup sugar
¼ cup vinegar
1 cup vegetable oil

Mix all the ingredients except the oil in a blender. Add oil very slowly while blending at high speed. Dressing will get thick. Let stand 24 hours before using.
   Serve in a small bowl letting guests spoon over fruit salad.

SEASONED SALT

Yield: About 1 Cup

1 cup salt
2½ teaspoons paprika
   (Hungarian)
2 teaspoons dry mustard
1 teaspoon curry powder
½ teaspoon or more of any of
   the following:
   thyme (dried)
   oregano (dried)
   sage
   garlic powder
   parsley (dried)
   onion powder
   rosemary (dried)

The basic mixture is salt, paprika, dry mustard, and curry powder. Add ½ teaspoon or more of thyme and oregano or any other particular herb in quantity according to your taste. Sieve or mix in blender.

Sprinkle on baked potatoes, scrambled eggs, rice, seafood salad, cucumbers, braised celery, or leeks. Excellent on green salads. Makes a good gift.

DRIED HERBS (Microwave)

Pick herbs in the morning after the dew has disappeared. Wash, if necessary. Blot dry on towels so there is no surface moisture. Place leaves between paper towels, and process in the microwave oven on high for 30 seconds to 1 minute. This varies with size and number of leaves. You may need to repeat one or two times for 30 seconds. This should give leaves a good green color and less flavor loss than conventional air drying. Place leaves in a dry place (conventional oven) overnight or for a few hours. Then place in a covered container.

Italian parsley dries especially well.

BREADS

ORANGE ROLLS

Yield: 2 Dozen

3 tablespoons butter
½ cup sugar
½ teaspoon salt
1 cup milk, scalded
1 package yeast, dry or cake
3 eggs, slightly beaten
3½ to 4 cups flour
    Rind of two oranges, grated
½ cup sugar
⅔ cup butter

Add butter, sugar, and salt to scalded milk and cool to lukewarm. Add yeast and eggs. Add sufficient flour to make a very soft dough. Beat or knead until smooth and elastic. Cover and let rise until double in bulk. Punch down, cover, and let rise a second time. Roll out about ¼ inch thick, and spread with filling of grated orange rind, sugar, and butter creamed together. Roll up as for jelly roll, and cut in 1-inch slices. Place cut side down in greased muffin pans. Cover; let rise until double in bulk. Bake at 400°F about 15 minutes.

Can be prepared in advance and refrigerated before baking. Can be frozen for a week or two after baking.

HONEY WHOLE WHEAT BREAD

Yield: 2 Loaves

1 cup milk
2 tablespoons sugar
1 tablespoon salt
¼ cup butter
½ cup honey
2 packages dry yeast
1½ cups warm water
2½ cups unbleached flour
5 cups unsifted
    whole wheat flour
1½ cups walnuts
2 tablespoons butter, melted

Heat milk until bubbles appear at the edge. Remove from heat. Add sugar, salt, ¼ cup butter, and honey; stir until butter melts. Cool to lukewarm. Dissolve yeast in warm water in large bowl. Stir in milk mixture. Add flours, all of the unbleached and 2½ cups of the whole wheat flour. Beat about 2 minutes until smooth. Add walnuts. Gradually add remaining flour, working with hands. Turn out on floured board. Let rest 10 minutes. Knead 10 minutes until smooth and elastic. Place in a large greased bowl; turn once and cover with a towel. Let rise in a warm place 1¼ hours. Punch down, divide in half, cover, and let rise 10 minutes. Shape into loaves, and place in greased pans. Brush tops with melted butter. Cover and let rise 1¼ hours. Bake at 400°F for 40 to 50 minutes.

INDIANAPOLIS COLLECTS & COOKS   147

CONTEMPORARY ART SOCIETY BUFFET IN HERRON HALL

Raw Vegetables with Olive Anchovy Sauce
Pasta Fettuccini
Salsa Alfredo
Salsa di Noci
Italian Bread Sticks
Sweet and Sour Spinach Salad
Italian Meringue Torte

FAILPROOF POPOVERS

Yield: 6

1 cup milk
1 cup unsifted flour
¼ teaspoon salt
2 unbeaten eggs

Place all ingredients in mixing bowl. Stir with a spoon until dry ingredients are moist. Mixture will be lumpy. Grease 6 cold glass custard cups, using ½ teaspoon butter for each. Fill with dough and put in cold oven. Bake 10 minutes at 450°F. Turn heat down to 350°F; bake 35 minutes, *do not open oven door.* Serve immediately with butter and jam.

PRALINE ROLLS

Yield: 32 Rolls

1 package dry yeast
¼ cup warm water
2¼ cups flour
2 tablespoons sugar
2 teaspoons baking powder
½ teaspoon salt
⅓ cup butter
⅓ cup scalded milk, cooled to lukewarm
1 egg
Topping and Filling
⅓ cup butter
¾ cup firmly packed brown sugar
½ cup chopped walnuts

Soften yeast in warm water. Sift together flour, sugar, baking powder, and salt into mixing bowl. Cut in butter until particles are fine. Stir in lukewarm milk, egg, and softened yeast. Mix well. Cream butter and brown sugar together until fluffy. Divide dough in half. Knead lightly on well-floured surface. Roll each half into a 9 x 12-inch rectangle. Spread each piece with ¼ of the sugar mixture. Sprinkle each with ¼ of the nuts. Roll up, starting with the 12-inch side. Cut each into 16 slices. Place on greased cookie sheets and flatten rolls somewhat. (Can be frozen at this point.) Spread each with ¼ of the sugar mixture and ¼ of the nuts. Cover and let rise in warm place. Bake at 425°F for 10 to 12 minutes.

Paul Jenkins, American, 1923-
PHENOMENA DANGER—PASS LEFT, 1964
oil on canvas, 51 x 76¾ inches
Gift of the Contemporary Art Society, 65.1

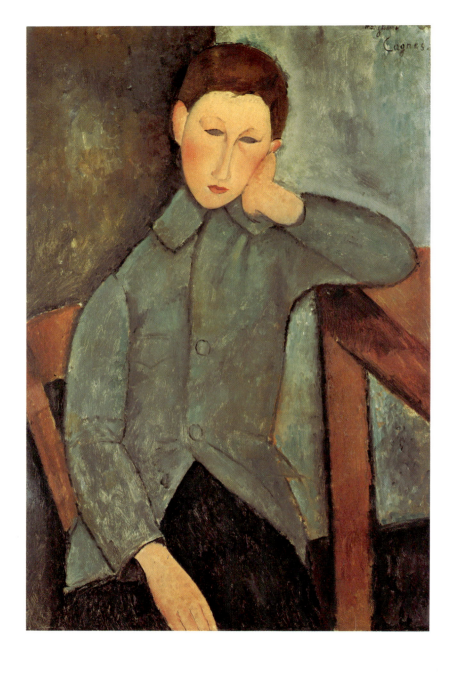

Amadeo Modigliani, Italian, 1884-1920
THE BOY, 1919
oil on canvas, 36¼ x 23¾ inches
Gift of Mrs. Julian Bobbs in memory of William Ray Adams, 46.22

Hans Hofmann, American, born Germany, 1880-1966
POEM D'AMOUR, 1962
oil on canvas, 36¼ x 48 inches
Gift of the Contemporary Art Society, 64.15

INDIANAPOLIS COLLECTS & COOKS   151

Richard Estes, American, 1936-
CAR REFLECTIONS, ca. 1968
acrylic on masonite, 48 x 30 inches
Purchased with Funds from the Penrod Society and
the National Endowment for the Arts, 71.207

MEXICAN CORNBREAD

Serves 6 to 8

1 cup whole wheat flour
1 cup cornmeal (yellow)
3 rounded teaspoons
   baking powder
½ teaspoon sea salt
½ to ¾ teaspoon chili powder,
   to taste
2 eggs, beaten
½ cup milk
½ cup unrefined corn germ oil or
   safflower oil
¼ cup finely chopped onion
½ cup finely chopped
   green pepper
1 jalapeño pepper, finely
   chopped OR ¼ teaspoon
   cayenne (optional)

Stir the flour, meal, baking powder, salt, and chili powder together in a large bowl. Add the eggs, milk, oil, onion, and peppers. Beat all ingredients together about 1 minute. Pour into an oiled 8 x 8-inch pan. Bake about 20 minutes at 425°F.

Good with sliced tomatoes, black bean soup, lentil soup, etc.

SCOTCH OATMEAL BREAD

Yield: 2 Loaves

1 cup milk
1 cup water
¼ cup cooking oil
½ cup molasses
1 cup old-fashioned oatmeal
1 tablespoon salt
2 packages yeast
1 cup whole wheat flour
3 cups unbleached white flour
1 tablespoon to ½ cup
   wheat germ (optional)

Scald milk, water, and cooking oil. Stir in the molasses, oatmeal, and salt and cool until lukewarm. Add yeast, whole wheat flour, and 1 cup unbleached white flour; then beat for 2 minutes. Slowly add rest of flour (beat with electric mixer as long as possible, then stir in the rest). As you start to knead the dough, add additional unbleached white flour, ½ cup at a time, until dough is no longer sticky. This may take from 2 to 2½ cups more unbleached flour as you knead. Knead about 10 minutes in all. Put in a warm, greased bowl; cover; let rise until double in bulk. Punch down; put in two greased loaf pans, and let rise a second time. Bake at 375°F for 25 to 35 minutes or until it sounds hollow when thumped with fingers. Cool on rack.

This is a firm, solid bread.

FRIED BISCUITS

Yield: 7 Dozen

1 quart milk
¼ cup sugar
½ cup shortening
2⅔ packages active dry yeast
6 teaspoons salt
7 to 9 cups flour

Warm milk to lukewarm. Add sugar. Dissolve shortening in milk; you may want to melt it separately for speed. Add yeast and salt. Stir well to mix. Work in the flour until a non-sticky consistency is reached. Knead until smooth and elastic. Place in greased bowl. Turn dough once to coat. Cover with towel. Let rise 1 to 1¼ hours. Drop by heaping teaspoonfuls into hot (350°F) fat to fry.

They puff up in cooking.

ITALIAN BREAD STICKS

Yield: 4 Dozen

3 cups flour
1 tablespoon sugar
1 teaspoon salt
4 tablespoons butter
1 cup lukewarm water
1 cake dry yeast, dissolved in
    ¼ cup warm water

Combine flour, salt, and sugar. Cut in the butter until it is the size of peas. Add water and dissolved yeast. Knead well. Let rise about 45 minutes. Punch down and divide into 4 parts. Roll out each part to about 12 inches. Cut this into 12 to 14 pieces. Roll or work each piece with hands until it is as thin as a lead pencil. Place on greased cookie sheet. Let rise 20 to 30 minutes. Bake at 400°F for 15 to 18 minutes.

Rolling dough very thin will give crisp and crunchy bread sticks. Thicker dough will give soft, chewy bread sticks.

ONION BREAD

Yield: 2 Loaves

1 package active dry or
  cake yeast
¼ cup warm water
1 cup sour cream or buttermilk
1 envelope onion soup mix
¼ teaspoon baking soda
2 tablespoons sugar
2 teaspoon salt
2 tablespoons butter, softened
3 eggs
1 cup warm water
4 to 6 cups sifted flour
  Sesame seeds

Sprinkle or crumble yeast into ¼ cup warm water to soften. In large bowl combine sour cream, soup mix, baking soda, sugar, salt, butter, 2 beaten eggs, and 1 cup warm water. Stir in softened yeast until smooth. Gradually add enough flour to form a stiff dough. Knead dough on floured board until smooth (about 5 minutes). Place in greased bowl, turning once to grease top. Cover with towel and let rise in warm place (80° to 85°) until double in bulk. Punch down. Divide in half. Form 2 loaves and place in greased loaf pans. Let rise in a warm place until light. Brush loaves with 1 beaten egg, and sprinkle with sesame seeds. Bake at 350°F for 40 to 45 minutes.
Freezes well. Delicious toasted.

LITTLE LOAVES WITH HERBS

Yield: 6 Miniature Loaves or a 9 x 5 x 3-inch Loaf

1¼ cups warm water (105°-115°F)
1 package or cake of yeast
2 tablespoons sugar
2 teaspoons salt
2 tablespoons butter
½ teaspoon basil
½ teaspoon thyme
½ teaspoon oregano
4 cups unsifted flour

Measure warm water into large, warm mixing bowl. Sprinkle or crumble in the yeast; stir until dissolved. Add sugar, salt, shortening, and herbs. Stir in 1½ cups of flour. Beat 2 minutes at medium speed on mixer. Scrape sides and bottom of bowl often. Stir in remaining flour. Blend with spoon until smooth, about 2 minutes. Cover; let rise about 1 hour in warm place until double in bulk. Stir down batter; spoon evenly into loaf pans. Cover. Let rise in warm place about 1 hour. Bake at 375°F for 45 minutes (less for small loaves).

Freezes well. Tasty for small sandwiches.

DILLY CASSEROLE BREAD

Yield: 1 Loaf

1 package dry yeast
¼ cup warm water
1 cup creamy cottage cheese
    (heated to lukewarm)
2 tablespoons sugar
1 tablespoon instant
    minced onion
1 tablespoon butter
1 tablespoon dill seed
1 teaspoon salt
¼ teaspoon soda
1 egg
2¼ to 2½ cups sifted flour

Soften yeast in water. Combine in mixing bowl the softened yeast, cottage cheese, sugar, onion, butter, dill seed, salt, soda, and egg. Add flour gradually to form a stiff batter, beating well after each addition. Cover. Let rise in warm place until light and double in size, about 50 to 60 minutes. Stir down batter. Turn into well-greased 8-inch round casserole (1½ to 2 quart). Let rise in a warm place until light, 30 to 40 minutes. Bake at 350°F for 40 to 50 minutes or until golden brown. Brush with soft butter and sprinkle with salt.

Breads

HERB CHEESE BREAD

Yield: 1 Large Loaf or 2 Small Loaves

1 cup warm water
1 package dry yeast
1 egg, room temperature
3 cups sifted flour
2 tablespoons sugar
1 teaspoon salt
3 tablespoons soft shortening
½ teaspoon basil
½ teaspoon oregano
Topping
½ lb. cheese, shredded
¼ cup minced onion
½ teaspoon oregano
½ teaspoon basil

Pour the warm water into a large mixing bowl and add the yeast. Let stand a few minutes, then stir to dissolve. Blend in the egg. Measure and blend the flour, sugar, salt, and shortening. Add half the flour mixture to the yeast. Start the mixer on medium speed and beat until smooth, 1½ to 2 minutes. Stop mixer. Add remaining flour and beat until the flour disappears and batter is smooth, about 1 to 1½ minutes. Scrape down batter from sides of bowl. Cover bowl with wax paper, and let rise in warm place until doubled, about 30 minutes. Meanwhile, grease one 11 x 7½-inch or two 8- or 9-inch square pans. Stir down batter in 20 to 24 strokes. Put into pans.

Topping: Combine cheese, onion, and herbs. Spread evenly over top of batter. Grease fingers and make dents with fingers on the topping, pressing almost to the bottom of the pan. Tap the pan on the table. Let batter rise in a warm place 20 to 30 minutes, no more than doubled. Bake at 375°F for 30 to 35 minutes or until golden brown. Remove from pans.

POVITIZA

Yield: 1 Bundt Loaf

1 cup butter
½ cup milk
2 packages dry yeast
¼ cup warm water
3 egg yolks
2½ cups sifted flour
¼ teaspoon salt
¼ cup sugar
2 cups chopped walnuts
1 teaspoon cinnamon
3 tablespoons sugar
½ cup chopped pitted dates
¾ cup milk
3 egg whites
1 cup sugar

Heat butter and milk together until butter is melted. Cool to lukewarm. In large bowl dissolve yeast in warm water, and beat in egg yolks. Blend in the cooled milk mixture. Sift in flour, salt, and ¼ cup sugar. Beat until smooth and creamy. Cover and refrigerate overnight. The next day blend walnuts, cinnamon, 3 tablespoons sugar, dates, and milk in saucepan. Cook over medium heat, stirring until thick, about 10 minutes. Remove from heat. Cool completely.

Beat egg whites until stiff. Slowly add 1 cup sugar, beating until meringue-like. Fold into the cooled walnut mixture. Remove dough from refrigerator, and cut into two equal parts. Dust each part with flour, and roll them out one at a time until they are circles 18 to 20 inches in diameter. Top each with half of the walnut mixture, spreading it to within 1 inch of the edge.

Roll up each like a jelly roll. (Work quickly with dough on a cold surface, as it softens quickly and is difficult to lift into pan. When placing in pan, make sure ends meet. Place top roll with the thickest part over the ends of the bottom roll so the over-all height is evened.) Use a well-greased Bundt pan, and let the dough rise for 30 minutes. Bake at 350°F for one hour, or until done. Let cool five minutes before removing from pan.

This freezes well. Can be reheated in foil.

Breads

POPPY SEED BREAD

Yield: 1 Large Loaf or 3 Small Loaves

2 cups sugar
1½ cups vegetable oil
4 eggs
1 teaspoon vanilla
3 cups flour
1½ teaspoons soda
1 large can Milnot
1 can poppy seeds: 3 oz.
1 small package walnuts,
    chopped (about ½ cup)

Mix together sugar, oil, eggs, and vanilla. Add flour, soda, Milnot, poppy seeds, and walnuts. Pour into a greased angel food cake pan or 3 small loaf pans. Bake at 350°F for 1 hour for large pan or 45 to 50 minutes if using small loaf pans.

PEANUT BUTTER STICKS

Yield: 50

1 loaf toasting white bread
1 cup peanut oil
1 cup peanut butter
1 box sesame seeds: 1.8 oz.
  Herb-flavored bread crumbs

Trim off bread crusts. Cut into strips ¾- to 1-inch widths. Toast in very slow oven, no higher than 250°F for 1 hour. Do not let sticks brown, only get dry. Dip sticks in mixture of peanut oil and peanut butter. Drain on cake racks, and put wax paper under the racks to catch drips. Toast sesame seeds until brown. *Do not use oil!* Watch carefully to prevent burning. Roll half of the strips in sesame seeds and the other half in herb-flavored bread crumbs.

    These freeze well and make a nice accompaniment for a vegetable or fruit salad luncheon.

INDIANAPOLIS COLLECTS & COOKS   159

BLUEBERRY MUFFINS

Yield: 16 to 20 Muffins

1 pint washed blueberries (may use frozen large berries)
6 tablespoons butter
1¼ cups sugar
2 large eggs
2 cups flour
½ teaspoon salt
2 teaspoons baking powder
½ cup milk
Topping
2 tablespoons sugar
¼ teaspoon cinnamon

Remove ½ cup of berries, crush with fork. Dry remaining berries in paper towel, reserve. Cream butter and sugar very well. Add eggs one at a time and beat well. Sift flour, salt, and baking powder together; add alternately with milk. Mix crushed berries with batter. Do not use mixer. Fold in whole berries. Fill greased muffin tins ⅞ full. Sprinkle with topping. (May use paper muffin tin liners.) Bake at 375°F for 30 minutes. Cool for 30 minutes.

BRAN MUFFINS

Yield: 48 Muffins

1 cup shortening
2 cups boiling water
2 teaspoons salt
3 cups sugar
4 eggs
2 cups All-Bran
4 cups 100% Bran
5 teaspoons soda
5 cups flour
1 quart buttermilk

Combine ingredients and store in a covered container in refrigerator for up to 6 weeks. *Do not stir* batter after it has been put in refrigerator. When ready to bake, fill greased muffin tins or paper baking cups in muffin tins ½ full, and bake at 400°F for 20 minutes.

Recipe may be halved. Make now and bake later.

Breads

ORANGE CRANBERRY NUT BREAD

Yield: 1 Loaf

2 cups sifted flour
1 cup sugar
1½ teaspoons baking powder
1 teaspoon salt
½ teaspoon baking soda
¼ cup shortening
1 teaspoon grated orange peel
¾ cup orange juice
1 egg, well beaten
1 cup cranberries, chopped
½ cup nuts

Sift together the dry ingredients. Cut in the shortening. Combine orange peel, orange juice, and egg; and add to the dry ingredients. Mix just enough to moisten. Fold in berries and nuts. Pour into a well-greased loaf pan. Bake in preheated oven at 350°F for 1 hour.

APRICOT NUT BREAD

Yield: 1 Loaf

1 can apricot nectar: 12 oz.
¾ cup chopped apricots
¾ cup raisins
1 egg, well beaten
½ cup sugar
1 tablespoon melted butter
2 cups sifted flour
2 teaspoons baking soda
½ teaspoon salt
⅓ cup milk
½ cup slivered almonds

Grease and flour a 9 x 5 x 2¾-inch pan. Mix nectar and fruits in a pan. Bring to a boil, and simmer for 5 minutes. Cool. Mix egg, sugar, and butter together. Mix together the dry ingredients, and add the milk alternately with the cooled fruit mixture. Stir well; add nuts. Bake in prepared pan for 1 hour at 350°F.
    Good for gifts.

RAISIN AND NUT FILLED COFFEECAKE

Yield: 3 Loaves

1 package dry yeast
¼ cup warm water
1 cup butter
3 tablespoons sugar
1 teaspoon salt
¾ cup milk
4¼ cups flour
3 eggs, separated
½ teaspoon vanilla
1 cup sugar
Filling
1 cup white raisins
⅓ cup brown sugar
1 cup chopped walnuts
1 teaspoon cinnamon

Soften yeast in ¼ cup warm water. Thoroughly cream butter, 3 tablespoons sugar, and salt. Add milk, 1 cup of flour, yeast mixture, egg yolks, and vanilla; beat well. Add 1¼ cups more flour; beat well. Gradually add remaining flour, using hands to mix, if necessary. Place in greased bowl; turn once to grease surface. Cover; let rise 2 hours. Punch down; divide into thirds. Let rest 10 minutes. Beat egg whites into soft peaks. Gradually add remaining 1 cup of sugar. Beat to stiff peaks. Roll out each portion of dough to an 8 x 10-inch rectangle, and spread each with ⅓ of the meringue to within one inch of the edges. Sprinkle each with ⅓ of the filling. Fold in half lengthwise. Pinch edges to seal. Bake at 350°F for 25 minutes. Cool on rack.

Drizzle with powdered sugar icing, if desired; or brush with 1 egg yolk beaten with 1 tablespoon milk before baking.

This freezes well.

Food Processor Instructions: Dissolve yeast in water in small bowl. Cream butter, sugar, and salt in processor. Add yolks, vanilla, milk, yeast mixture, and 1 cup of flour. Blend 5 seconds. Add 1 cup of flour, process 5 seconds. Add another cup of flour scraping sides. Empty bread onto counter, and knead in remaining flour. Place in greased bowl and continue as above.

TOASTED ALMOND ANISE LOAF

Yield: 1 Loaf

2¼ cups sifted flour
 2 teaspoons baking powder
 ½ teaspoon salt
 ½ cup butter
 1 cup sugar
 ¾ cup chopped almonds,
   toasted
 ½ teaspoon anise seed
 ¼ teaspoon almond extract
 5 eggs, beaten

Sift together the flour, baking powder and salt. Cream together the butter and sugar. Add the flour mixture and almonds. Stir in the anise seed, almond extract, and the beaten eggs. Turn into a well-greased 9 x 5 x 3-inch loaf pan, lightly floured on the bottom only. Bake 50 to 60 minutes at 350°F.

This is a nice tea bread spread with cream cheese. It is also good toasted.

LEMON BREAD

Yield: 2 Loaves

⅔ cup melted butter
2½ cups white sugar
 4 eggs
 ½ teaspoon almond flavoring
 ½ teaspoon lemon flavoring
 3 cups flour
 2 teaspoons baking powder
 1 teaspoon salt
 1 cup milk
 1 cup chopped nuts
 2 tablespoons grated
   lemon peel
Topping
 6 tablespoons lemon juice
 ¼ cup sugar

Grease two 8 x 4 x 2½-inch loaf pans, line with wax paper on the bottom. Blend butter and sugar. Beat in eggs one at a time. Add extracts. Sift dry ingredients; add to egg mixture alternately with milk. Blend just enough to mix; don't overbeat. Fold in nuts and lemon peel. Pour into prepared pans. Bake at 325°F about 1 hour or until loaves test done. Combine lemon juice and sugar, and pour over hot loaves as soon as they come from the oven. Cool 10 minutes and remove from pans.

This is a sweet, lemony, cake-like bread that freezes well. Nice for gift giving.

SPICED APPLESAUCE BREAD

Yield: 1 Loaf

1 cup applesauce
1 cup sugar
½ cup vegetable oil
2 eggs, beaten
3 tablespoons milk
2 cups flour
1 teaspoon soda
½ teaspoon baking powder
½ teaspoon cinnamon
¼ teaspoon salt
¼ teaspoon nutmeg
¼ teaspoon allspice
½ cup chopped pecans
Topping
¼ cup chopped pecans
¼ cup brown sugar
½ to ¾ teaspoon cinnamon

Combine applesauce, sugar, oil, eggs, and milk. Mix well; then add the flour, soda, baking powder, spices, and nuts. Mix well and pour into a greased loaf pan. Combine the topping ingredients, and sprinkle over unbaked loaf, pressing into batter slightly. Bake at 350°F for 1 hour or until done.

Best served hot, but also good the second day. Serve with a salad luncheon or light supper. Also delicious for breakfast with coffee. It may be frozen. Wonderful for gifts.

KUCHEN

Yield: 1 Bundt Cake

3 to 4 cups flour
1¼ cups sugar
½ teaspoon salt
2 packages dry yeast
½ cup butter, softened
1 cup very hot water
4 eggs, room temperature
1 tablespoon grated lemon peel
¼ teaspoon nutmeg
    Powdered sugar

Grease and flour a 10-inch Bundt or tube pan. In large bowl mix 1 cup flour, sugar, salt, and yeast. Add butter. Grandually add water and beat with mixer for 2 minutes on medium speed. Add eggs and 1 cup flour, and beat 2 minutes on high speed. Cover and let rise for one hour. Batter will not be doubled. Stir in lemon peel and nutmeg and enough of remaining flour to make a thick dough. Beat in with a spoon. Pour into prepared pan. Cover and let rise until doubled, about 1 hour. Bake at 350°F for 40 minutes or until done. Remove from pan and cool on rack. Sprinkle with powdered sugar.

Makes a slightly sweet dinner bread or rather plain coffeecake.

Breads

BUTTER PECAN CRUMB CAKE

Serves 12 to 16

½ cup firmly packed
  brown sugar
½ cup flour
½ teaspoon cinnamon
¼ cup butter, softened
1 package yellow cake mix:
  2 layer size
1 package butter pecan flavor
  instant pudding-pie filling
  mix: 3½ oz.
1 cup sour cream: ½ pint
⅓ cup oil
4 eggs
½ teaspoon maple extract
  (optional)

Grease and flour a 10-inch tube pan. Combine brown sugar, flour, and cinnamon in small bowl. Cut in butter to make crumbs; set aside. Combine remaining ingredients in large mixer bowl. Blend; then beat at medium speed for 4 minutes. Pour into prepared pan. Bake at 350°F for 50 minutes. Carefully remove partially baked cake from oven, and sprinkle immediately with crumb mixture. Bake 10 to 15 minutes longer or until cake tester inserted in center comes out clean and cake begins to pull away from sides of pan. Do not underbake. Cool in pan 10 minutes. Carefully remove from pan; finish cooling with crumb side up on rack.

This resembles a pound cake and can be sliced very thin, served with fruit, ice cream, or just plain.

WHOLE WHEAT WAFFLES OR PANCAKES

Yield: 12 Medium Pancakes or 4 Large Waffles

2 eggs
1 cup milk
1 tablespoon brown sugar
1 tablespoon vegetable oil
1 cup whole wheat flour
1 teaspoon baking powder
½ teaspoon salt

Separate eggs and beat whites until stiff, then beat yolks until fluffy. Add milk to yolks, and mix well. Add remaining ingredients and mix until well blended only. Fold in beaten egg whites, and bake in waffle grill.

For pancakes, do not separate eggs, follow same instructions.

Isabel Bishop, American, 1902-
TIDYING UP, 1941
oil on masonite, 15⅛ x 11⅝ inches
Delavan Smith Fund, 43.24

DESSERTS

SPICED PERSIMMON PUDDING

Serves 12 to 16

2 cups persimmon pulp:
   1 qt. sieved
2 cups sugar
2 eggs, beaten
1½ teaspoons cinnamon
½ teaspoon nutmeg
½ teaspoon ground cloves
2 cups flour
¼ teaspoon baking soda
1 teaspoon salt
4 cups milk
Sauce
 ½ cup sugar
 2 tablespoons flour
 2 tablespoons butter
  Cinnamon
  Nutmeg
 ¾ cup water

Grease a 9 x 12-inch pan. Add sugar, eggs, and spices to pulp. Sift flour, soda, and salt. Add to pulp alternating with milk. Beat until smooth. Pour into prepared pan. Bake 1 hour at 350°F. Cool and cut into squares. (Pudding goes down as it cools.) Serve with whipped cream or Sauce.

Sauce: Combine sugar, flour, butter, and cinnamon and nutmeg to taste with water; cook over medium heat until thick. Cool and serve over Spiced Persimmon Pudding.

SWEDISH CRÈME

Yield: 1 Quart

1 pint heavy cream
1 cup sugar
1½ teaspoons gelatin
1 pint sour cream
1 teaspoon vanilla

Mix heavy cream, sugar, and gelatin. Heat until gelatin is dissolved. Cool sightly. Add sour cream and vanilla. Refrigerate until chilled.

This is a delicious topping for fresh fruit as it stays "fluid" and does not set up.

ALLIANCE COFFEE IN CLOWES COURTYARD

Praline Rolls
Orange Rolls
Lemon Bread
Bran Muffins
Bite-sized Fresh Fruits and Cheeses
Tea
Coffee

BAKED LEMON PUDDING

Serves 6 to 8

3 tablespoons butter
1 cup sugar
3 egg yolks, well beaten
1 lemon, grated rind and juice
3 tablespoons flour
1½ cups milk
3 egg whites, stiffly beaten

Butter and sugar an 8- or 9-inch square pan or a 2-quart round pan. Cream butter and sugar until soft and smooth; add well-beaten egg yolks, grated rind, and lemon juice; mix. Add flour; then milk. Mix well. Fold in egg whites. Pour into prepared baking pan. Set in a pan of hot water, and bake at 350°F for 45 minutes. A delicate cakelike layer forms on top and the pudding supplies its own sauce. Serve either warm or cool.

A very pleasant luncheon dessert. Nice for serving in hot weather.

COLD RASPBERRY SOUFFLÉ

Serves 6 to 8

4 teaspoons gelatin
3 tablespoons cold water
Salt
2 packages frozen raspberries, thawed: 10 oz. each
1 tablespoon lemon juice
½ cup sugar
3 egg whites
1 cup whipping cream, whipped

Soften gelatin in cold water with a pinch of salt; heat and dissolve. Purée berries. Add gelatin, lemon juice, and sugar. Place over ice, stirring often, until thickened. Beat egg whites until stiff. Fold into berry mixture, then fold into whipped cream. Chill.

Serve dotted with whipped cream and fresh berries or almonds.

Desserts

Peter Paul Rubens, Flemish, 1577-1640
TRIUMPHANT ENTRY OF CONSTANTINE INTO ROME, ca. 1622
oil on panel, 19 x 25½ inches
The Clowes Fund Collection

Joseph Mallord William Turner, English, 1775-1851
EAST COWES CASTLE, THE SEAT OF J. NASH, ESQ.,
THE REGATTA BEATING TO WINDWARD, 1828
oil on canvas
Gift of Mr. and Mrs. Nicholas Noyes, 71.32

Anthony van Dyck, Flemish, 1599-1641
THE ENTRY INTO JERUSALEM, 1617-1618
oil on canvas, 59½ x 90¼ inches
Gift of Mr. and Mrs. Herman C. Krannert, 58.3

Willem Kalf, Dutch, 1619-1693
STILL LIFE WITH BLUE JAR, 1669
oil on canvas, 30¾ x 26 inches
Gift of Mrs. James W. Fessler in memory of Daniel W. and Elizabeth C. Marmon, 45.9

MAPLE SYRUP MOUSSE

Serves 8 to 10

1½ cups milk
2 envelopes gelatin
3 eggs, separated
1 cup pure maple syrup
1 cup heavy cream

Pour the milk into a heavy saucepan, and sprinkle with gelatin to soften. This takes considerably longer than over water, about 15 minutes. Place over moderate heat, and stir until gelatin dissolves. Remove from heat. Beat egg yolks until thick. Stir in a little of the hot milk; then combine the two, beating together with a wire whisk. Whip in the maple syrup. Refrigerate until the mixture just begins to set. Beat the egg whites with electric mixer until they hold firm, shiny peaks. Add the maple syrup mixture to the whites, and beat vigorously with a wire whisk. Beat cream until it just holds a soft shape. Combine and pour into a 1-quart mold. Seal surface with plastic wrap and refrigerate. When firm, turn out of mold onto a serving dish.

Serve on a Lace Cookie or in a dessert dish with a dollop of sweetened whipped cream. Pass a pitcher of maple syrup. May be prepared a day ahead.

PERSIMMON PUDDING

Serves 8

1 cup brown sugar
1 cup milk
¼ teaspoon salt
⅓ stick butter, melted
2 cups flour
1 teaspoon baking soda
2 cups persimmon pulp

Grease an 8-inch square baking pan. Combine brown sugar, milk, salt, and butter. Mix flour and soda and add the persimmon pulp which has been put through a sieve. Turn into the prepared pan. Bake at 325°F for 60 to 75 minutes.

Serve plain or with ice cream or whipped topping.

INDIANAPOLIS COLLECTS & COOKS 173

WINE JELLY (Gelée du Vin)

Serves 8

2 tablespoons gelatin
¼ cup cold water
¾ cup boiling water
½ cup sugar
1¾ cups orange juice
6 tablespoons lemon juice
1 cup sherry or dry white wine

Soak the gelatin in ¼ cup cold water. Dissolve it in boiling water. Stir in the sugar until dissolved. Cool these ingredients; add the two juices and the wine. Pour into a 4-cup mold. Chill until firm.

Serve with whipped cream, if desired.

LEMON SHERBET (Frappé)

Serves 8

Grated rind of 1 lemon
¾ cup lemon juice: 3 to 4
lemons
2 cups sugar
½ teaspoon lemon extract
3 cups milk
1 cup whipping cream

Combine lemon rind, lemon juice, sugar, and extract in a large bowl. Stir well. Stir in the 3 cups of milk. Whip the cream in a deep bowl until stiff. Fold in the lemon mixture. Pour the sherbet into a shallow pan such as an 11 x 13-inch baking dish. Place in freezer and stir three times in the first hour as the sherbet freezes. Sherbet may be stored in a plastic container or served that day.

This is especially good with green crème de menthe.

RHUBARB BREAD PUDDING

Serves 6

3 cups diced firm bread
4 cups diced rhubarb
1 cup sugar, to taste
½ teaspoon cinnamon
½ teaspoon nutmeg,
freshly ground
¼ cup butter, melted

Mix all ingredients together, and pour into buttered 1½-quart casserole. Bake uncovered at 375°F for 40 minutes.

This may be served with whipped cream or ice cream.

CALIFORNIA FRUIT SOUP

Serves 8

1 cup dried apricots
1 cup pitted prunes
5 cups water
1 can orange juice:
    6 oz. condensed
Rind of one lemon,
    yellow part only
1 cinnamon stick: 3 inch
2 tablespoons tapioca,
    quick-cooking
½ cup sugar
1 tablespoon lemon juice
½ cup sour cream
¼ cup shredded orange rind

Combine apricots, prunes, water, and orange juice in saucepan and let stand 30 minutes. With sharp knife pare bright yellow part of lemon rind and add to fruits. Add cinnamon, tapioca, and sugar. Simmer, covered, 10 minutes. Add 1 tablespoon lemon juice. Remove lemon peel. Cool. Chill and serve in chilled bowls garnished with sour cream and orange rind.

APPLE CRUMB PUDDING

Serves 4 to 6

3 large tart apples
⅓ cup sugar
1 cup flour
1 cup light brown sugar
1 cup finely chopped pecans
    (optional)
½ cup butter
½ teaspoon cinnamon
    Whipped cream

Butter an 8-inch pie pan. Peel, core, and thinly slice apples. Line prepared pan with one-half of the apple slices; sprinkle with ⅓ cup sugar, and cover with remaining apples. Combine flour, brown sugar, and pecans. Cream butter and work it into this mixture. Add cinnamon and mix well. Spread mixture evenly over apples, pressing down at edges and cutting several gashes for steam to escape. Bake at 350°F for 40 to 50 minutes. Serve warm with whipped cream.

One-fourth cup of raisins may be mixed with the apples.

INDIANAPOLIS COLLECTS & COOKS

PUMPKIN FLAN

Serves 8

¾ cup sugar
1 cup canned pumpkin
1 cup milk
1 cup cream
6 eggs, slightly beaten
½ cup sugar
½ teaspoon salt
2 teaspoons vanilla
⅓ cup brandy

In a large iron or heavy gauge aluminum skillet, cook ¾ cup sugar over low heat until it melts and makes a light brown syrup. Immediately pour into a heated 8-inch or 1½-quart baking dish. Rotate the dish quickly to coat the side and bottom completely. In the top of a double boiler combine the pumpkin, milk, and cream. Cook over hot water until thoroughly scalded. Beat eggs slightly; add ½ cup sugar, salt, vanilla; and then gradually, the hot pumpkin mixture. Add brandy and pour into prepared dish. Bake 50 to 60 minutes at 325°F in a pan of hot water which reaches halfway up the baking dish. Flan is done when a silver knife inserted in the center comes out clean. Refrigerate overnight. When ready to serve, run a spatula around the edge to loosen and invert on a shallow dish.

POTS-DE-CRÈME

Serves 5 to 6

1 cup semi-sweet chocolate bits
1 egg
2 tablespoons sugar
1½ teaspoons vanilla
Pinch of salt
¾ cup less 2 teaspoons
scalded milk

Blend all ingredients in an electric blender. Do not boil milk, but it must be hot enough to melt chocolate in blender. Process for 1 minute or until chocolate bits have been melted. Pour into pots-de-crème or custard cups and refrigerate until set. Best set overnight, but can be used in 4 hours.

This will keep several days in the refrigerator.

Desserts

PERSIMMON SPANISH CRÈME

Serves 4

2 cups milk
1 tablespoon gelatin
2 egg yolks
⅓ cup sugar
⅛ teaspoon salt
½ teaspoon vanilla
   Approximately 1 pint persimmon pulp
2 egg whites

Scald the milk with the gelatin. When the gelatin is dissolved, add to the 2 egg yolks which have been mixed with the sugar and the salt. Stir and cook over very low heat until it forms a coating on spoon. Cool; add the vanilla. Reserve half of the custard and half of the persimmon pulp. Layer the other half in parfait glasses, alternating the custard and persimmon pulp. Beat 2 egg whites until stiff, and fold into the reserved custard. Add a layer of this mixture to the parfait glasses, and top with the reserved persimmon pulp. Refrigerate several hours.

Giovanni Francesco Romanelli, Italian, 1610-1662
THE FINDING OF MOSES, ca. 1658
oil on canvas
Gift of the Alliance of the Indianapolis Museum of Art, 72.18

COLD ORANGE SOUFFLÉ

Serves 8

1 envelope gelatin
¼ cup cold water
1 teaspoon freshly grated
   orange rind
½ cup fresh orange juice
4 eggs, separated
½ teaspoon salt
1 cup granulated sugar
1 cup heavy cream

Make a brown paper collar on a 1½ quart soufflé dish, or use a 2-quart dish. Sprinkle gelatin into cold water to soften. In double boiler or heavy saucepan combine egg yolks, juice, salt, and ½ cup sugar. Cook, stirring constantly until thickened and custardy. Stir in gelatin and orange rind. Turn into large bowl. Cool, but do not chill. Beat egg whites until they hold stiff peaks while adding the remaining ½ cup sugar gradually. Whip cream stiff. Gently fold whites into orange mixture. Fold in whipped cream until completely blended. Pour into soufflé dish. Refrigerate for at least three hours.

Recipe may be doubled.

RHUBARB REFRESHER

Serves 6 to 8

1 lb. rhubarb
½ cup water
1 cup sugar
1 envelope gelatin
2 teaspoons lemon juice
2 cups whipped topping,
   thawed

Cook rhubarb in ¼ cup water and the sugar until it strings. Soften gelatin in ¼ cup water, and add to the hot rhubarb. Stir well until gelatin is dissolved. Remove from heat and add lemon juice. Cool until the mixture begins to set and mounds slightly. Fold in whipped topping, and turn into a 1-quart mold. Chill until firm.

Garnish with fresh strawberries. A light dessert, nice for warm weather.

WALNUT TORTE

Serves 12 to 16

12 eggs, separated
   (room temperature)
1½ cups sugar
 3 tablespoons flour
2½ cups grated black walnuts

Grease well and flour three 9-inch cake pans. Line bottom of pans with wax paper, and grease and flour paper. Separate eggs and beat egg yolks for five minutes. Gradually add sugar, beating well after each addition. Add flour and grated nuts. Beat egg whites until stiff. Fold gently into above mixture. Pour into prepared pans. Bake at 350°F for 25 to 30 minutes, or until done. Cool slightly and remove from pans. Frost with Walnut Torte Frosting.

WALNUT TORTE FROSTING

Yield: Frosting for Three 9-inch Cake Layers

1½ cups unsalted butter
1½ teaspoons vanilla
 ½ teaspoon rum
 2 eggs, separated
 1 cup plus 2 tablespoons sugar
⅓ cup water
¾ cup grated black walnuts

Cream together the butter, vanilla, and rum. Add two well-beaten egg yolks. Set aside. Combine sugar and water in a saucepan with a tight-fitting lid, and boil gently with lid on for 5 minutes. Using a candy thermometer continue boiling until soft ball stage of 240°F. Beat egg whites until stiff. Add syrup slowly to egg whites and cool. Beat in egg and sugar mixture, 2 tablespoons at a time, to butter mixture. Last of all add the grated walnuts. Chill until just cool, and then frost the Walnut Torte.

INDIANAPOLIS COLLECTS & COOKS

DREAM BARS

Yield: 35 Bars

½ cup butter
1 tablespoon sugar
1 cup flour
2 eggs
1 cup light brown sugar
2 tablespoons flour
½ teaspoon baking powder
1 cup nuts
½ cup coconut
1 teaspoon vanilla
4 tablespoons butter
2 cups powdered sugar
1 teaspoon vanilla
2 tablespoons cream, or
    enough for spreading
    consistency

Grease a 6 x 8-inch pan. Cream butter and sugar in electric mixer at low speed. Add flour and mix an additional minute. Press mixture into prepared pan. Bake at 350°F for 10 to 15 minutes. Mix eggs, brown sugar, flour, baking powder, nuts, coconut, and vanilla in electric mixer on low. Pour this mixture over the first mixture, and bake at 350°F for about 25 minutes. Let cool. Cream the butter, powdered sugar, vanilla, and cream; and spread over the cooled cake. Cut into bars.

PRALINES

Yield: 2 Dozen

24 graham crackers
1 cup brown sugar
1 cup butter
1 cup broken pecans

Place graham crackers on cookie sheet with sides. Put sugar and butter in saucepan. Bring to a slow rolling boil, stirring constantly. Remove from heat and add pecans. Put 1 tablespoon of mixture on each graham cracker. Bake at 325°F for exactly 10 minutes. Remove and cool for 10 minutes before lifting from cookie sheet.
    Quick and easy!

Desserts

LACE COOKIES

Yield: 40 Cookies

½ cup unsalted butter, melted
¾ cup brown sugar, packed or
   white sugar
3 tablespoons sifted flour
½ teaspoon salt, scant
1 teaspoon baking powder
1 teaspoon vanilla
1 cup quick oats
1 egg, beaten

Mix all ingredients together. Drop ½ teaspoonfuls every 3 inches on buttered and *floured* cookie sheet. Bake 7 minutes at 350°F. Wave sheet twelve times before removing cookies with pancake turner.

Lovely with Maple Syrup Mousse or ice cream. Freezes well.

POPPY SEED TORTE

Yield: 9-inch Pie

Crust
   2 cups graham cracker crumbs
   ¾ cup brown sugar
   ½ cup melted butter
Filling
   2 cups milk
   ½ cup poppy seeds
   3 tablespoons cornstarch
   ½ cup sugar
   ⅛ teaspoon salt
   3 egg yolks
   1 teaspoon vanilla
Meringue
   3 egg whites
   6 tablespoons sugar

Combine the graham cracker crumbs, sugar, and melted butter until well mixed. Reserve ½ cup of mixture. Spread remaining in a 9-inch pie pan. Set aside.

Filling: Scald milk in double boiler. Combine poppy seeds, cornstarch, sugar, and salt. Add to milk and boil for 5 minutes, stirring constantly. Beat egg yolks; add slowly to custard, and boil 5 minutes more. Add vanilla. Cool. Pour into crumb crust and top with meringue.

Meringue: Beat egg whites until frothy. Add sugar 1 tablespoon at a time, beating well after each addition. Beat until stiff. Sprinkle with reserved ½ cup crumbs. Bake at 300°F to 325°F for 30 to 35 minutes.

PEANUT BUTTER PIE

Serves 8

1 package cream cheese: 8 oz.
½ cup crunchy peanut butter
1 cup powdered sugar
½ cup milk
1 carton frozen non-dairy
    topping, thawed: 9 oz.
1 graham cracker crumb or
    baked pie shell, 9-inch
¼ cup finely chopped peanuts

Whip cream cheese until soft and fluffy. Beat in peanut butter and sugar. Slowly add milk, beating until well blended. Fold topping into mixture. Ladle into pie crust and sprinkle with peanuts. Freeze until firm. Remove from freezer 5 to 10 minutes before serving. Do not thaw before serving.

OATMEAL PIE

Yield: 2 Pies

1½ sticks butter
1½ cups sugar
 4 eggs, beaten
 2 teaspoons salt
1½ cups corn syrup
1½ cups quick oats
 1 cup coconut
 2 unbaked pie shells

Cream together the butter and sugar. Add the beaten eggs. Mix together the salt, corn syrup, oats, and coconut. Add to first mixture, and pour into two unbaked pie shells. Bake at 350°F for 35 to 40 minutes.
    This is a very rich pie, similar to pecan pie in flavor.

LEMON SQUARES

Yield: 50 1-inch Squares

1 cup butter, softened
2 cups flour
½ cup powdered sugar
Filling
 4 eggs
 2 cups sugar
 6 tablespoons lemon juice
 1 tablespoon flour
½ teaspoon baking powder
 1 cup chopped pecans

Thoroughly mix butter, flour, and powdered sugar. Press into a 10 x 13-inch pan. Bake 15 minutes at 325°F.
    Filling: Beat the eggs until light, and add the remaining ingredients. Pour on top of baked pastry. Bake at 325°F for 45 minutes. Cool. Sprinkle with powdered sugar.

Desserts

COCONUT-BUTTERMILK PIE

Yield: 9-inch Pie

1½ cups sugar
3 eggs
¼ cup butter, melted
½ cup coconut, unsweetened
  (or more, to taste)
½ cup buttermilk
1 tablespoon flour
1 teaspoon vanilla
1 unbaked pie crust: 9-inch

Use mixer to mix sugar and eggs. Add cooled melted butter, and stir in remaining ingredients. Pour into unbaked pie crust. Bake at 350°F for 45 to 55 minutes.

CHOCOLATE CHEESECAKE

Serves 20

2 packages chocolate wafer
  cookies: 8½ oz. each
½ teaspoon cinnamon
½ cup butter, melted
1 cup sugar
4 eggs
1½ lb. cream cheese
1 lb. semi-sweet chocolate
1 teaspoon vanilla
2 tablespoons cocoa
3 cups sour cream
¼ cup butter, melted

Crush chocolate wafers and mix with cinnamon and melted butter. Press firmly into a 10-inch spring form pan. Chill. Mix the sugar and eggs, and beat until light and fluffy. Add softened cream cheese gradually, beating well after each addition. Melt chocolate and add to egg mixture along with vanilla, cocoa, and sour cream. Add melted butter. Mix well. Pour into chilled shell, and bake at 350°F for 45 minutes. Chill overnight.
  A rich delicious dessert.

MARBLE CHEESECAKE

Serves 16 to 20

Crust
1½ cups graham cracker crumbs
 ¼ cup sugar
 6 tablespoons butter, melted
Filling
 4 packages cream cheese:
  8 oz. each
 2 teaspoons vanilla
1¾ cups sugar
 6 eggs
 2 cups light cream
 2 squares unsweetened
  chocolate, melted

Combine and press in bottom and 2 inches up the sides of a 9-inch spring form pan.
 Beat cream cheese and vanilla to blend. Add sugar. Add eggs one at a time, mixing well. Stir in cream. Combine 3 cups of batter with cooled chocolate. Pour plain cheese mixture into crust. Add chocolate mixture using zig-zag motion, but allow spots of chocolate instead of just thin lines. Bake at 450°F for 15 minutes. Reduce heat to 300°F, and contine baking 1 hour and 10 minutes. Cool 1 hour and remove from pan. Chill.

PRALINE CHEESECAKE

Serves 12 to 16

20 graham crackers,
  finely crushed
 6 tablespoons melted butter
 ⅓ cup sugar
 3 packages cream cheese:
  8 oz. each
1¼ cups dark brown sugar,
  packed
 2 tablespoons flour
 3 eggs
1½ teaspoons vanilla
 ½ cup chopped pecans

Mix crumbs, butter, and sugar together, and press into a 9-inch spring form pan. Bake at 350°F for 10 minutes. Combine cream cheese, brown sugar, and flour and mix well. Add eggs, one at a time, beating well after each addition. Blend in vanilla and pecans. Pour mixture over crumb crust. Bake at 300°F for 60 minutes. Cool and loosen from pan. Brush with maple syrup and garnish with pecan halves.
 This cheese cake is very rich and may be cut in smaller portions to serve more people.

Desserts

GINGERBREAD RING

Serves 6 to 8

½ cup butter
1½ cups brown sugar
1 egg, well beaten
1½ cups flour
1 teaspoon soda
1 teaspoon ginger
1 teaspoon cinnamon
½ teaspoon ground cloves
⅛ teaspoon salt
½ cup molasses
½ cup boiling water
Hot Butterscotch Sauce
1 cup brown sugar
2 tablespoons flour
⅛ teaspoon salt
½ cup milk
½ cup water
2 tablespoons butter
½ teaspoon vanilla

Butter and flour a tube or Bundt cake pan. Cream together butter and brown sugar. Add beaten egg. Sift together flour, soda, spices, and salt. Mix molasses with boiling water. Add the dry ingredients alternately with the molasses to the sugar and butter mixture. Bake in prepared pan at 350°F for 30 to 40 minutes. Remove from pan; cool.

Hot Butterscotch Sauce: Blend dry ingredients, and add milk and water gradually. Stir until blended. Add butter and vanilla, and cook 2 to 4 minutes, stirring constantly. Serve warm. Sauce may be refrigerated and reheated in a double boiler.

Gingerbread Ring may be served with whipped cream or ice cream in addition to the Hot Butterscotch Sauce.

BANANA CAKE

Yield: 8-inch Layer Cake

Cake
¾ cup butter
1½ cups sugar
2 eggs
1 cup mashed, very ripe
   bananas
2 cups sifted flour
1 teaspoon baking soda
   Pinch of salt
½ cup sour cream
½ cup chopped English walnuts
Butterscotch Frosting
½ cup brown sugar
½ cup butter
2½ tablespoons evaporated milk
2 (or more) cups powdered
   sugar

Grease and flour two 8-inch cake pans. Cream butter and sugar together. Add unbeaten eggs and beat until fluffy. Add bananas and blend. Sift together flour, soda, and salt. Add alternately with the sour cream. Fold in the nuts. Bake in prepared cake pans at 350°F for 30 minutes. When cool, cover with Butterscotch Frosting.

Butterscotch Frosting: Combine brown sugar, butter, and evaporated milk in pan. Bring to a boil. Put into a small mixer bowl. Add confectioners' sugar gradually, while mixer is set on slow speed. Blend until mixture is of good spreading consistency. Double recipe for thicker frosting.

The unfrosted cake freezes well.

BROILED FROSTING

Yield: Covers 9 x 13-inch Cake

¾ cup butter
1½ cups brown sugar
1½ tablespoons cream
1 teaspoon vanilla
1½ cups coconut
1 cup finely chopped pecans

Combine butter, sugar, cream, and vanilla in a heavy saucepan. Heat gently over a low fire until soft and thick, stirring constantly. Add coconut and pecans. Spread on warm cake. Put under the broiler, about 4 or 5 inches from heat, until frosting bubbles and barely starts to brown. This burns easily, so watch carefully.

Good on Oatmeal Cake.

Desserts

ITALIAN CREAM CAKE

Serves 16

1 cup butter
2 cups sugar
5 egg yolks
2 cups flour
1 teaspoon baking soda
1 cup buttermilk
1 teaspoon vanilla
3½ oz. flaked coconut
½ cup chopped pecans
5 egg whites, stiffly beaten
Icing
8 ounces cream cheese,
softened
¼ cup butter
1 lb. powdered sugar
1 teaspoon vanilla
½ cup chopped nuts

Cream butter; add sugar and beat until mixture is smooth. Add egg yolks and beat well. Sift flour, measure, and sift again with the soda. Add alternately with buttermilk to creamed mixture. Stir in vanilla, coconut, and chopped pecans. Fold in egg whites. Pour batter into greased and floured 9 x 13-inch pan. Bake at 350°F for 45 to 50 minutes. When cake is cool, cut in half. Fill and frost with icing. Refrigerate until serving time.

Icing: Beat cheese and butter until smooth. Add sifted sugar; mix well. Mix in vanilla and chopped nuts.

OATMEAL CAKE

Yield: 9 x 13-inch Cake

1¼ cups boiling water
1 cup rolled oats
1 cup sugar
1 cup brown sugar
½ cup shortening
2 eggs
1⅓ cups flour
1 teaspoon baking soda
1 teaspoon baking powder
½ teaspoon salt
1 teaspoon cinnamon
½ teaspoon nutmeg
1 teaspoon vanilla

Pour boiling water over rolled oats. Set aside. Cream together the sugars and the shortening. Beat in eggs, one at a time. Sift flour, soda, baking powder, salt, and spices together. Whip oatmeal mixture with creamed mixture. Add vanilla. Add sifted dry ingredients, stirring just enough to mix. Turn into a greased and floured 9 x 13 x 2-inch pan. Bake in a preheated oven at 350°F for 30 to 35 minutes. Top with Broiled Frosting.

This is an easy and delicious cake for picnics or casual parties.

INDIANAPOLIS COLLECTS & COOKS

ITALIAN MERINGUE TORTE (Marengo Cavour)

Serves 10 to 12

4 egg whites
½ teaspoon cream of tartar
1 cup sugar
1 teaspoon vanilla
1 teaspoon instant coffee
  powder
4 tablespoons coffee-flavored
  liqueur
2 cups whipping cream
8 ounces small chocolate bars,
  coarsely chopped

Grease and flour 2 baking sheets. In a large mixing bowl combine the egg whites and cream of tartar. Beat just until frothy. Add sugar, 1 tablespoon at a time, every 30 seconds. Add vanilla and beat for 2 more minutes. The whites should hold very stiff, sharp peaks. Trace an 8-inch circle on each baking sheet; spread half of meringue mix on each, leaving one smooth, one with peaks and swirls. Place in pre-heated 250°F oven just above and just below the center of the oven, and switch sheets after 1 hour. Continue baking for ½ hour more. Color will be white to pale amber. Turn off heat and leave meringues in closed oven for 3 more hours. Remove while still warm; flex pan to pop meringues free, but cool to room temperature on pan. (Disks may be stored airtight as long as five days.)

Filling: Mix instant coffee powder and coffee-flavored liqueur. Beat whipping cream until stiff. Fold in the coffee mix and the chopped chocolate bars. Place the plain meringue disk on a flat serving plate. Spread whipped cream evenly on just the top of the disk. Place the decorative meringue disk on the whipped cream. Cover and refrigerate 8 hours or overnight.

This is a simple and elegant dessert.

PLUMGOOD CAKE

Yield: 7½ x 12-inch Cake

½ cup butter
2 tablespoons shortening
1 cup sugar
2 eggs
3 cups flour
2 teaspoons baking powder
½ teaspoon salt
⅓ cup canned milk
1 teaspoon vanilla
½ cup sugar
1 teaspoon cinnamon
2 cans Italian plums
   (prune plums)

Grease a 7½ x 12-inch pan well. Cream butter and shortening. Add sugar and cream well. Add eggs and blend together. Mix together flour, baking powder and salt. Add to creamed mixture alternately with milk and vanilla. Batter will be heavy. Pat half of this batter in greased pan, wetting hands first to aid in making it smooth. Cut plums into quarters or eighths and spread over batter. Combine sugar and cinnamon, and sprinkle half of it on top of plums. Add other half of batter, and sprinkle top with remaining half of sugar and cinnamon. Bake at 350°F for 35 minutes or until brown. Cool before cutting.

Other fruits may be used.

SEEDLESS GRAPE DESSERT

Serves 6

2 lbs. seedless grapes:
   6 to 8 cups
¼ cup brandy
½ cup whipping cream
½ cup sour cream
2 tablespoons powdered sugar
  Dark brown sugar

Remove stems from grapes. Place grapes in shallow serving dish. Sprinkle with brandy; turn the grapes to coat evenly. Whip cream. Combine with sour cream and powdered sugar. Blend. Pour cream mixture over grapes; then sprinkle with brown sugar. Place in freezing compartment for about 10 minutes to chill.

Quick and easy.

INDIANAPOLIS COLLECTS & COOKS

COCOA COLA CAKE

Serves 9

½ cup butter
¼ cup miniature marshmallows
2 tablespoons cocoa
½ cup cola drink
1 cup sugar
1 cup flour
½ teaspoon baking soda
1 egg, beaten
¼ cup buttermilk
Frosting
¼ cup butter, melted
2 tablespoons cola drink
2 tablespoons cocoa
1½ cups powdered sugar
Chopped nuts, optional

Grease an 8-inch square baking pan. In a saucepan melt the butter and marshmallows. Add cocoa and cola, and stir on low heat until blended. Mix together the sugar, flour, and baking soda. Stir butter mixture into sugar mixture and beat to blend. Add beaten egg and buttermilk, mixing just to blend. Pour mixture into prepared pan. Bake at 350°F for 40 minutes. Cool before frosting.

Frosting: In saucepan melt butter;stir in cola and cocoa and blend. Add sugar until mixture is of spreading consistency and beat thoroughly. Frost cooled cake and sprinkle with nuts, if desired.

This is a very rich, moist, and delicious cake.

BLUEBERRY SOUP

Serves 6 to 8

1 pint blueberries
2 cups water
½ cup sugar
1 cinnamon stick: 3 inch
¼ teaspoon nutmeg
1 lemon, sliced thin,
    including skin
2 cups sour cream
½ cup dry red wine (Burgundy)

Wash and drain blueberries. Combine with water, sugar, cinnamon, nutmeg, and lemon. Bring to boil and simmer, uncovered, 15 minutes. Strain the mixture. Discard the pulp. Chill. Just before serving, beat in sour cream and wine.

DRESSED BANANAS

Serves 8 to 10

½ to ¾ cup sugar
2 tablespoons butter
1 egg, well beaten
1½ tablespoons vinegar
3½ tablespoons water
6 to 8 bananas
Crushed peanuts (without skins or hulls)

Mix all ingredients except bananas and peanuts and heat. Stir constantly until mixture coats a spoon. Chill. Slice bananas and put a layer of them in a salad bowl. Cover bananas with dressing, then a layer of crushed peanuts over dressing. Repeat until bowl is filled.

May also be served on bibb lettuce as a salad. Beautiful in a crystal bowl.

PUMPKIN ROLL

Serves 12

3 eggs
1 cup sugar
⅔ cup canned pumpkin
1 teaspoon lemon juice
¾ cup cake flour
1 teaspoon baking powder
2 teaspoons cinnamon
1 teaspoon ginger
½ teaspoon grated nutmeg
½ teaspoon salt
¾ cup finely chopped walnuts
Powdered sugar
Filling
1 cup powdered sugar
4 tablespoons butter
6 ounces cream cheese
½ teaspoon vanilla

Grease a 15 x 10 1-inch jelly roll pan. Line with wax paper and grease and flour. Beat eggs 5 minutes. Gradually add sugar; stir in pumpkin and lemon juice. Sift together the flour, baking powder, cinnamon, ginger, nutmeg, and salt; gently fold into the pumpkin mixture. Spread the batter on the prepared pan, and sprinkle with the chopped nuts. Bake at 375°F for 15 minutes. Remove from oven and turn cake onto towel dusted with powdered sugar. Remove wax paper from cake. Roll the cake up in the towel immediately. Beat filling ingredients until smooth. When cake is lukewarm, unroll and spread with filling, leaving a 1-inch margin. With the aid of the towel, roll the cake. Wrap in wax paper and refrigerate overnight.

INDIANAPOLIS COLLECTS & COOKS 191

CHOCOLATE CHERRY CAKE

Yield: 9 x 13-inch Cake

1 package chocolate cake mix:
   19 oz.
2 eggs, beaten well
1 teaspoon almond or
   rum flavoring
1 can cherry pie filling: 1 lb.
Frosting
   ¼ cup butter, softened
1½ tablespoons cocoa
   ½ teaspoon vanilla
   ½ lb. powdered sugar
   Milk as needed

Grease and flour a 9 x 13-inch cake pan. Combine the cake mix, eggs, and flavoring. Gently fold in the cherry pie filling by hand, being careful not to crush the whole cherries. Pour into prepared pan, and bake at 350°F for 40 minutes. Cool and frost.

Frosting: Combine all ingredients, adding milk to make a nice spreading consistency.

This is a moist cake that keeps well. It also may be frozen.

PEACHES AND CREAM CHEESE CAKE

Serves 6 to 8

¾ cup flour
1 teaspoon baking powder
½ teaspoon salt
1 package vanilla pudding
   (not instant): 3 oz.
3 tablespoons butter, softened
1 egg
½ cup milk
1 can sliced peaches: 16 oz.
8 ounces cream cheese,
   softened
½ cup sugar
3 tablespoons reserved
   peach juice
1 tablespoon sugar
½ teaspoon cinnamon

Grease a deep dish 9-inch pie pan. Mix together the flour, baking powder, salt, pudding mix, butter, egg, and milk. Pour into greased pan. Place drained fruit on top of batter. Beat cream cheese, sugar, and reserved juice for 2 minutes. Spoon over fruit. Mix together sugar and cinnamon and sprinkle over cake. Bake at 350°F for 30 to 35 minutes.

May be served warm or cold. Delicious leftover for breakfast!

PEACHES WITH SHERRY SAUCE

Serves 6

6 fresh peaches, halved
Butter
½ teaspoon brown sugar for each peach half
3 macaroons
Sherry Sauce
1½ tablespoons sugar
3 egg yolks
½ cup good sherry

Make Sherry Sauce and refrigerate. Place fresh peach halves in baking dish, cut sides up. Put a dot of butter and ½ teaspoon brown sugar in each hollow. Crumble half a macaroon over each peach; press down into the butter. Refrigerate peaches, if they are prepared in advance. When ready to serve, bake peaches at 350°F for 30 minutes. Serve hot with very cold sauce!
Sherry Sauce: Add sugar to the egg yolks. Beat until light, gradually adding the sherry. Cook in top of double boiler over hot, not boiling, water. Stir constantly until thick and smooth. Chill until very cold.
   Delicious summertime dessert. So easy!

George Ortman, American, 1926-
M, 1969
acrylic on shaped canvas, 83⅛ x 72 inches
Nell Clarke Herrington Memorial Fund, 70.69

CRÈME BRÛLÉE CAJUN

Serves 4

4 ripe, unblemished peaches
   of top quality
1 cup sugar
2 cups water
1 teaspoon vanilla
1 cup heavy cream
2 eggs
2 tablespoons sugar
   Dash of salt
½ cup brown sugar
½ teaspoon vanilla

Plunge the fresh peaches in boiling water for 1 to 2 minutes. Slip off skins, cut in half, and remove seeds. Combine the sugar, water, and vanilla. Bring to boil and cook for 10 minutes. Place peach halves in syrup, reduce heat and simmer gently until fruit is just tender. Remove with slotted spoon, and place in baking dish.

Scald cream in top of double boiler over simmering water. Beat together the eggs, sugar, and salt. Pour scalded cream over egg mixture gradually. Return mixture to double boiler, and cook until as thick as medium white sauce, stirring constantly (5 to 6 minutes). Remove from heat and add vanilla. Pour custard over poached peaches. Chill well. One hour before serving, place the baking dish in a large pan filled with crushed ice. Sprinkle with brown sugar (that has been "sifted" by forcing through strainer) over the top of the custard. Place under the broiler about six inches from the heat. Brown the sugar until melted, taking care not to burn it. Watch carefully! Serve warm or cold.

This is an elegant dessert which can be done in individual bakers also. Canned peaches may be substituted for fresh.

RELISHES, PICKLES, AND JELLIES

BASIL JELLY

Yield: Four 8-ounce Jars

1 cup basil leaves, tightly
    packed
2 cups water
2 tablespoons white wine
    Vinegar
    Salt
3½ cups sugar
3 ounces liquid pectin

Put basil in large saucepan. Crush well. Add water and bring to a boil for 30 seconds. Remove from heat, cover, and let stand for 15 minutes. Strain 1½ cups liquid into large saucepan, and add vinegar, salt, and sugar; bring to a hard boil, stirring. Add pectin; return to a hard boil. Boil one minute and remove from heat. Skim off foam. Pour into sterile jars leaving ⅛-inch headspace. Seal at once with paraffin or sterile 2-piece lids.

Nice on crackers with cream cheese. Delightful with lamb, steak, or roast beef.

SPICY CRANBERRY RELISH

Yield: 4 Cups

4 cups cranberries
1 cup seedless raisins
1⅔ cups sugar
1 tablespoon cinnamon
1½ teaspoons ginger
¼ teaspoon cloves
1 cup water
¼ cup chopped onion
1 medium apple,
    pared and chopped
½ cup thinly sliced celery

Combine cranberries, raisins, sugar, cinnamon, ginger, cloves, and water in a large saucepan. Cook 15 minutes until berries pop and mixture thickens. Stir in onion, apple, and celery; simmer 15 minutes longer or until mixture is thick. Cool and refrigerate.

Good with poultry and pork.

Some of the recipes in this section are old family favorites. If you are unfamiliar with home canning, please consult a recent edition canning book.

HOT PEPPER JELLY

Yield: 12 8-ounce Jars

3 large bell peppers,
  cut and seeded
12 hot jalapeño peppers,
  not seeded
⅓ cup water
3 cups cider vinegar
5 lbs sugar
2 packages pectin: 6 oz. each
  Green food coloring

Pulverize peppers in water in a blender. Put in a very large cooking pot, and add other ingredients, except pectin and food coloring. Boil hard for 5 minutes. Remove from heat. Skim. Add pectin and 2 or 3 drops of food coloring. Pour immediately into sterile glasses, and seal with sterile lids.

Serve as hors d'oeuvres spooned over cream cheese with crackers.

Hot!

BAKED APPLE BUTTER

Yield: 1 Quart

4 cups unsweetened
  applesauce
1 lb. dark brown sugar
⅓ cup cider vinegar
¼ teaspoon cloves, ground
¾ teaspoon cinnamon

Combine in a 2-quart casserole or roaster. Bake uncovered for 2½ to 3 hours at 325°F or until apple butter is thick and glossy. (Mixture will thicken more when chilled.) Stir occasionally, increasing frequency as cooking time increases. All ingredients may be altered to suit individual taste without impairing the product. May be canned or refrigerated.

APRICOT CHUTNEY

Yield: 2½ Quarts

1 can apricot halves: 29 oz.
2 cups dark brown sugar
2 cups distilled vinegar
1 cup chopped onions
1 cup golden raisins
½ cup crystallized ginger,
  minced
2 tablespoons mustard seeds
1 teaspoon chili powder
1 teaspoon salt
1 garlic clove, minced
1 teaspoon ground cloves

Drain and dice the apricots, reserving the syrup. Heat the reserved syrup and the remaining ingredients to boiling. Reduce the heat to simmer, and cook, uncovered, 45 minutes. Stir in the apricots; simmer, uncovered, 45 minutes. Pour into sterilized quart jars, leaving ½-inch space, and seal; or just pour into jars and keep refrigerated.

This is delicious over cream cheese as an hors d'oeuvre with unsalted crackers. It is also a good condiment with curries.

Relishes, Pickles, and Jellies

SUNCHOKE PICKLES (Jerusalem Artichokes)

Yield: 3 Pints

2 lbs. sunchokes
1¼ cups salt
2 cups brown sugar
1 teaspoon turmeric
2 teaspoons mustard seeds
2 small onions
2 cups apple cider vinegar
1 teaspoon pickling spice

Scrape sunchokes carefully with a vegetable brush. Soak overnight in water and salt and a tiny bit of vinegar to keep them from turning dark. Drain, rinse in clear water, peel, and chop fine or grate. Peel and quarter onions, and cut in small thin slices. Bring remaining ingredients to a boil for 5 minutes. Pour over vegetables. Pack in hot sterilized jars. Seal with paraffin.

WOODLAND FARMS DILLED CARROTS

Yield: 8 pints

4 lbs carrots
4½ cups water
4 cups distilled vinegar
½ cup kosher salt
Few drops red pepper
   seasoning
8 cloves garlic
8 teaspoons dill weed

Wash carrots and pare if necessary. Cut into 4-inch sticks, and pack into hot pint jars. Combine water, vinegar, salt, and red pepper seasoning in large saucepan. Bring to boil. Lower heat and simmer 5 minutes. Ladle into jars, leaving ¼-inch headroom. Add 1 clove garlic and 1 teaspoon dill to each jar. Seal and process 10 minutes in hot water bath. Store at least two weeks to develop flavors.
   Wonderful!

SPICED PECANS

Yield: 2 Pounds

2 lbs. pecans
2 egg whites
2 tablespoons water
2 cups sugar
2 teaspoons cinnamon
2 teaspoons salt

Beat egg whites and water until frothy. Add pecans and stir well. Mix the sugar, cinnamon, and salt. Fold into nut mixture until nuts are well coated. Bake on a buttered cookie sheet at 250°F for 1 hour, stirring every 15 minutes.
   Delicious for holiday time.

APPETIZERS
Cold
Caviar Pâté   23
Cheese Mousse   6
Chester Cakes   6
Chutney Curry Spread   8
Cottage Cheese Bourbon Dip   10
Crab or Shrimp Mold   9
Crab Meat Spread   23
Cream Cheese with Chutney Dip   2
Curry Dip for Vegetables   10
Dilled Salmon Mousse   69
Hungarian Cheese   7
Mushrooms à la Grecque   3
Marinated Mushrooms   4
Marinated Onions and Bleu Cheese   8
Molded Liverwurst Spread   24
Nova Scotia Salmon Mold   21
Pâté de Foie à la Crème   25
Pâté Miniatures   24
Savory Beef Stuffed Cherry Tomatoes   17
Seafood Mousse   20
Shrimp with Mustard Sauce   22
Spiced Cocktail Cheese   7
Spiced Pecans   197
Spinach Dip   11
Stuffed Cucumbers   17
Tarragon Shrimp Sauce   103
Tomato Cheese Spread   8
Vermouth Liver Pâté   26
Water Chestnut Spread   7
Hot
Artichoke Appetizer   11
Baked Mushrooms with Bleu Cheese   2
Baked Shrimp Dip   22
Broiled Mushroom Canapes   3
Cheese Puffs   4
Cheese Triangles   5
Crab Meat Quiche   9
Deep Fried Vegetables   18
Fried Camembert Hors D'Oeuvres   1
Golden Chicken Nuggets   19
Hot Artichoke Dip   11
Hot Mushroom Dip   2
Hot Sweet and Sour Sauce for Avocados   103
Midget Hamburgers   10
Mushroom-filled Pastry   1
Parmesan Cheese Leaves   12
Sausage Balls   20
Sweet and Sour Cocktail Meatballs   18
Zucchini Appetizers   19
BREADS
Apricot Nut Bread   161
Blueberry Muffins   160
Bran Muffins   160
Butter Pecan Crumb Cake   165
Dilly Casserole Bread   156
Failproof Popovers   148
Fried Biscuits   154
Herb Cheese Bread   157
Honey Whole Wheat Bread   147
Italian Bread Sticks   154
Küchen   164
Lemon Bread   163
Little Loaves with Herbs   156

Mexican Cornbread   153
Onion Bread   155
Orange Cranberry Nut Bread   161
Orange Rolls   147
Peanut Butter Sticks   159
Poppy Seed Bread   159
Povitiza   158
Praline Rolls   148
Raisin and Nut Filled Coffee Cake   162
Scotch Oatmeal Bread   153
Spiced Applesauce Bread   164
Toasted Almond Anise Loaf   163
Whole Wheat Waffles   165
BRUNCH, LUNCH, AND SUPPER
Artichoke Casserole with Crab or Chicken   71
Baked Turkey Sandwiches   51
Black-eyed Peas and Pot Likker   64
Brunch Eggs   58
Cheese Soufflé   57
Chutney Chicken Salad   134
Crab Sandwiches   52
Crab Meat Quiche   9
Creamed Eggs   58
Curried Chicken Salad   133
Curried Eggs with Shrimp Sauce   59
Denver Brunch Sandwich   50
Mushroom Mousse with Sauce Suprème   68
Mushroom Stroganoff   61
Noodles with Pesto   65
Onion Pie   62
Pasha   60
Pasta Fettuccini   66
Poz Noz   60
Presnutz   57
Salsa Alfredo   67
Salsa di Noci   67
Shrimp and Shell Salad   59
Skillet Split-Pea Dinner   63
Spinach Crêpes with Ham and Cheese   64
Spinach and Ham Roll-Ups   63
Swedish Creamed Mushrooms   61
Swiss Pumpkin Shell Supper   47
CAKES
Banana Cake   186
Broiled Frosting   186
Chocolate Cheesecake   183
Chocolate Cherry Cake   192
Cocoa Cola Cake   190
Gingerbread Ring   185
Italian Cream Cake   187
Italian Meringue Torte   188
Marble Cheesecake   184
Oatmeal Cake   187
Peaches and Cream Cheese Cake   192
Plumgood Cake   189
Poppy Seed Torte   181
Praline Cheesecake   184
Pumpkin Roll   191
Walnut Torte   179
Walnut Torte Frosting   179
COFFEE CAKES
Butter Pecan Crumb Cake   165
Raisin and Nut Filled Coffee Cake   162
Küchen   164

COOKIES
Dream Bars   180
Lace Cookies   181
Lemon Squares   182
Pralines   180

DESSERTS
Apple Crumb Pudding   175
Baked Lemon Pudding   168
Blueberry Soup   190
California Fruit Soup   175
Cold Orange Soufflé   178
Cold Raspberry Soufflé   168
Crème Brûlée Cajun   194
Dressed Bananas   191
Lemon Sherbet   174
Maple Syrup Mousse   173
Peaches with Sherry Sauce   193
Persimmon Pudding   173
Persimmon Spanish Crème   177
Pots-de-Crème   176
Pumpkin Flan   176
Rhubarb Bread Pudding   174
Rhubarb Refresher   178
Seedless Grape Dessert   189
Spiced Persimmon Pudding   167
Swedish Crème   167
Wine Jelly   174

ENTRÉES
Accompaniments
Mustard Mold   100
Pineapple Dressing   101
Spiced Fruit with Port   102
Yorkshire Pudding   100
Meats
Asparagus Ham Bake   91
Barbecued Beef   51
Bavarian Pot Roast   82
Beef Salami   78
Beef Vinaigrette   80
Ham Loaf   90
Hungarian Goulash   81
Italian Sausage   90
Korean Flank Steak   79
Lamb Stew   86
Neapolitan Beef   83
North Italian Sausage   78
Onion or Pepper Steak   80
Polish Style Pork Rolls   88
Pork Chops in Wine   87
Pork Tenderloin Deluxe   91
Sausage Balls   20
Sausage Loaf   89
Spanish Steak   79
Spiced Corned Beef   82
Spinach Crêpes with Ham and Cheese   64
Spinach and Ham Roll-Ups   63
Stewed Rabbit or Chicken   87
Sweet and Sour Cocktail Meatballs   18
Sweet and Sour Pork   92
Teriyaki Flank Steak   85
Veal in Lemon-Wine Sauce   84
Veal Marsala   85
Veal with Tarragon   84

Poultry
Artichoke Casserole with Crab or Chicken   71
Baked Chicken with Wine   96
Baked Turkey Sandwiches   51
Barbecued Chicken with Honey Glaze   98
Basque Chicken   94
Chicken Chaufroid   99
Chicken Fricassee   89
Chicken in the Old Style   99
Chicken Pie   102
Chicken Roquefort Sandwich Filling   48
Chicken with Forty Cloves of Garlic   97
Chicken with Garlic and Lemon   96
Chutney Chicken Salad   134
Cobb Salad   134
Curried Chicken Salad   133
Golden Chicken Nuggets   19
Herb Chicken Casserole   93
Hot California Chicken Salad Sandwich   48
Oven Chicken Salad   98
Rolled Chicken Washington   95
Spanish Chicken   93
Stewed Rabbit or Chicken   87
Turkey with Orange Rice   101
Seafood
Artichoke Casserole with Crab or Chicken   71
Crab Meat and Wild Rice Strata   70
Crab Meat Quiche   9
Crab or Shrimp Mold   9
Dilled Salmon Mousse   69
Dorothy's Fish Sauce   104
Nova Scotia Salmon Mold   21
Roquefort and Shrimp Stuffed Sole   72
Seafood Mousse   20
Scallops in Vermouth   71
Shrimp and Shell Salad   59
Shrimp Eggplant Casserole   77
Shrimp Étouffée   77
Shrimp with Mustard Sauce   22
Tarragon Shrimp Sauce   103
Trout Amandine   70

MENUS
Brunch   72
Buffet   148
Cocktail Party, GALA   12
Coffee   168
Dinner—Spring   32
Dinner—Fall   108
Luncheon   52
Picnic   128

PIES
Coconut Buttermilk Pie   183
Oatmeal Pie   182
Peanut Butter Pie   182

RELISHES, PICKLES, AND JELLIES
Apricot Chutney   196
Baked Apple Butter   196
Basil Jelly   195
Hot Pepper Jelly   196
Spiced Pecans   197
Spicy Cranberry Relish   195
Sunchoke Pickles   197
Woodland Farms Dilled Carrots   197

SALADS
Arabian Oranges   143

Artichoke Rice Salad   133
Blueberry Salad   143
Broccoli Salad   136
Chicken Chaufroid   99
Chutney Chicken Salad   134
Cobb Salad   134
Curried Chicken Salad   133
Fresh Mushroom Salad   137
Garden Relish Tray   136
Hearty Cheese Salad   139
Herbed Tomatoes   140
Hot Baked Potato Salad   138
Molded Asparagus Salad   135
Molded Spinach Salad   139
Pea and Peanut Salad   138
Pickled Beet Gelatin Salad   141
Roquefort Mousse Salad   143
Shrimp and Shell Salad   59
Strawberry Mold   142
Sweet and Sour Spinach Salad   139
Tabbouleh   145
Tomartichokes   135
Tomato Surprise   141
Watercress-Mushroom Salad   137
Zucchini Salad   140

SALAD DRESSINGS
Celery Seed Fruit Salad Dressing   145
Dried Herbs   146
German Potato Salad Dressing for Endive   144
Poppy Seed Dressing   144
Seasoned Salt   146
Vinaigrette à l'Italienne Dressing   144

SANDWICHES
Barbecued Beef   51
Baked Turkey Sandwiches   51
Chicken Roquefort Sandwich Filling   48
Crab Sandwiches   52
Denver Brunch Sandwich   50
Hot California Chicken Salad Sandwich   48
Spiced Mustard Sauce   103
Tuna Swiss Special   50

SAUCES
Dorothy's Fish Sauce   104
Honey Almond Sauce for Vegetables   104
Hot Sweet and Sour Sauce for Avocados   103
Olive Anchovy Sauce   104
Salsa Alfredo   67
Salsa di Noci   67
Spiced Mustard Sauce   103
Tarragon Shrimp Sauce   103

SOUPS
Avocado Soup   29
Black Bean Soup   31
Black-eyed Peas and Pot Likker   64
Borscht with Sour Cream   39
Brandy Cheddar Soup   28
Cauliflower Soup   49
Chicken Avocado Soup   30
Chilled Mushroom Shrimp Bisque   40
Corn Chowder   39
Cream of Broccoli Soup   37
Cream of Sorrel Soup   43
Creamy Celery Spinach Soup   52

Crème Mushroom Olga   40
Creole Bean Soup   29
French Onion Soup   42
Fresh Tomato Soup   45
Gazpacho   38
Green Soup   32
Hearty Fall Vegetable Bean Soup   30
Hot Tomato Starter   45
Lentil Soup   27
Mulligatawny   27
New England Fish Chowder   28
Slim Vegetable Soup   32
Spring Scallion Soup   44
Summer Green Tweed Soup   38
Sunchoke Purée   44
Swiss Pumpkin Shell Supper   47
Tomato Soup   46

VEGETABLES
Artichoke Appetizer   11
Asparagus with Sauce   127
Baked Cauliflower   116
Baked Eggplant   117
Baked Eggplant Creole   117
Baked Spinach and Artichokes   121
Bright Green Broccoli   106
Broccoli Casserole   106
Cabbage and Eggplant in Cheese Sauce   114
Carrots or Parsnips and Cabbage   115
Celery Amandine   116
Cheddar Zucchini Bake   123
Curry Dip for Vegetables   10
Deep Fried Vegetables   18
Green Rice   113
Green Vegetable Casserole   125
Grits Casserole   125
Herbed New Potatoes   108
Hot Artichoke Dip   11
Honey Almond Sauce for Vegetables   104
Mushroom and Cheese Zucchini   118
Mushrooms and Cream   118
Mushrooms and Zucchini in Wine Sauce   120
Peppers Roquefort   107
Raisin Sauced Beets   105
Rice Cakes   107
Rice Ring Maria   121
Saffron Rice   107
Savory Sweet Peppers   108
Skillet Potato Salad   113
Smothered Cabbage Wedges   115
Spinach Dip   11
Spinach with Fresh Cream   119
Spinach and Rice Casserole   120
Spiced Sweet Potatoes   122
Squash Parmesan   122
Stuffed Cucumbers   17
Summer Squash Casserole   122
Swedish Creamed Mushrooms   61
Sweet and Sour Bean Casserole   125
Tomato Onion Cheese Casserole   105
Tomatoes with Bacon and Olives   127
Wild Rice with Mushrooms   119
Yugoslavian Vegetable Casserole   128
Zucchini Appetizer   19
Zucchini Casserole   123

We wish to thank all of the following people who aided in the production of this cookbook by contributing recipes, testing, typing, proofreading, art selection, or editing. Those who assisted as chairmen or co-chairmen of committees are marked with an asterisk.

Abrams, Mrs. Jerome J.
Acheson, Mrs. Donald
Albea, Mrs. Charles M.
Allison, Miss Mae
Alsdorf, Mrs. James W.
Appel, Mrs. John C.
Arceneaux, Mrs. Andre
Armstrong, Mrs. Richard S.
Atkins, Mrs. Thomas

Bassett, Mrs. Walter D.
Backer, Mrs. Herbert J.
Bagal, Mrs. S.
Barker, Mrs. E. A.
Barr, Mrs. Roy Kenneth
Bates, Mrs. Robert S.
Battersby, Mrs. J. S.
Bauer, Miss Rea D.
Baxter, Charles
Baxter, Mrs. Richard V.
Beck, Mrs. Evart M.
Behrman, Mrs. R. D.
Bennett, Mrs. Paul A.
Bergerson, Mrs. L. J.
Berry, Mrs. Thomas J.
Berte, Mrs. Lawrence
Bindner, Mrs. George M.
Bourdo, Mrs. Jon J.
Bourke, Mrs. Leon H.
Bowman, Mrs. Donald E.
Boyd, Mrs. Nelson A.
Boyer, Mrs. Victor L.
Boyle, Mrs. Richard D.
Bradford, Mrs. W. J.
Bradley, Mrs. C. Harvey, Jr.
Bridgford, Mrs. Oral W.
Bruner, Mrs. Larry J.
Buchholtz, Mrs. William L.
Bugher, Mrs. M. A.
Bulger, Mrs. Thomas R.
Burns, Mrs. David V.
Burns, Mrs. John E., Jr.
*Burns, Mrs. Ralph M.
Butler, Mrs. John L.
*Butz, Mrs. Stephen C.
Butz, Mrs. William A.

Cahn, Mrs. Peter H.
Cain, Mrs. Joseph E.
Canfield, Mrs. Carl R., Jr.
Carlton, Mrs. Robert W.
Carroll, Mrs. Alex S.
Cederquist, Mrs. S. G.
Chambers, Mrs. Robert W.
*Charbonneau, Mrs. George C.
Chernish, Mrs. Stanley
Cherrington, Mrs. Robert M.
Childress, Mrs. Don
Clark, Mrs. Lawrence L.
Clark, Mrs. Lawson J.
Clowes, Allen W.
Cohen, Mrs. Sultan G.
Cole, Mrs. Ralph M.
Cox, Mrs. Lester W.
Cravens, Mrs. Joseph C.
Crowder, Mrs. D. L.
Crowe, Mrs. Thomas K.

Dailey, Mrs. Orville
Daily, Mrs. Wilson S.
Dankert, Mrs. W. L.
Dean, Mrs. Donald F.

DeBoest, Mrs. Henry F.
Deckelbaum, Mrs. W. S.
DeLance, Mrs. Robert
DeRose, Mrs. Robert A.
DeVoe, Miss Lucille
Dominianni, Mrs. Samuel J.
*Doughty, Mrs. Samuel R., Jr.
Dussinger, Mrs. James
Dutton, Mrs. C. B.
Dutton, Mrs. Stephen J.
Dyer, Mrs. William A., Jr.

Easton, Mrs. Nelson R.
Eaton, Ms. Jo
Eiteljorg, Mrs. Harrison
Eiteljorg, Mrs. Roger S.
Elder, Mrs. Bowman
Elder, Mrs. Donald F.
*Eldridge, Mrs. Gail
Elliott, Mrs. Michael M.
Elting, Mrs. Hal E.
Erganian, Mrs. George

Fansler, Mrs. Michael D.
Fay, Ms. Carolyn
Fehsenfeld, Mrs. John
Ferree, Mrs. Joseph W.
Ferreira, Mrs. Paul F., Jr.
Fletcher, Mrs. Gale
Fortune, Mrs. Robert P. O'R.
Foust, Mrs. Omer
Fox, Mrs. Marvin J.
Frey, Mrs. Hugh W.
Fritzke, Mrs. Bernhardt C.

Gadbury, Mrs. James A.
Gardner, Mrs. James S.
*Garrett, Mrs. David A.
Gelpke, Mrs. Roy A.
*Gibson, Mrs. Richard K.
Gibson, Mrs. William E.
Gilfoy, Peggy S.
Glasser, Mrs. Richard L.
Goldberg, Mrs. S. C.
Goldsmith, Mrs. Jerrold K.
Goodyear, Mrs. John
Graham, Ms. Mitzi K.
*Greenleaf, Mrs. Robert W.
Greer, Mrs William J.
Greist, Mrs. John H.
Grosz, Mrs. Hanus J.
Gruen, Mrs. Robert
Guio, Mrs. Victor

Haesloop, Mrs. Robert E.
Hamra, Miss Pauline
Hanley, Mrs. Ann Fuller
Harman, Mrs. Harry J.
Harper, Mrs. H. Thomas
Harrison, Mrs. William R.
Hartley, Mrs. William G.
Hartnett, Mrs. George
Hathaway, Mrs. Max
Hays, Mrs. Will H., Jr.
Hebert, Mrs. Henry O.
Helmen, Mrs. Charles H.
Henderson, Mrs. Jane R.
Hessler, Alice J.
Hiatt, Mrs. Frank T.
Hickam, Mrs. John B.
Hicks, Mrs. David A.
Hillman, Mrs. Gentry

Hobbs, Mrs. John W., III
Hockert, Mrs. Chester
Holland, Ms. Patricia A.
Holmes, Ms. Virginia H.
Hoog, Mrs. George H.
Hoppock, Mrs. David W.
Horn, Mrs. Robert
Horst, Mrs. George W.
House, Mrs. George C.
Hudson, Mrs. Terrell G.
Hunter, Mrs. Charles A.
Hurwitz, Mrs. Roger

Jackson, Mrs. Louise
Jameson, Mrs. Booth T.
Janson, Dr. Anthony
Jerden, Mrs. Ardis E.
Johnson, Mrs. Robert A.
Johnston, Mrs. R. Cameron
Jones, Dr. Elizabeth M.
Jones, Ms. Terry
Judd, Mrs. Robert H.

Kahlo, Mrs. E. Havens
Kahn, Mrs. Alexander
Kaufman, Mrs. Ford
King, Mrs. Harold
Knapp, Mrs. Dean L.
Knapp, Mrs. George R.
Kortepeter, Fred
Kossoy, Mrs. Aaron D.
Kramer, Mrs. Donald L.
Krause, Martin F., Jr.
Krieg, Mrs. Peter
Kuerst, Mrs. Alfred E.
Kuhn, Mrs. George A., Jr.

Lachen, Mrs. Suzanne Y.
Lanagan, Mrs. John B.
Lange, Mrs. Philo B.
Larick, Mrs. Harry C.
Lautzenheiser, Mrs. A. D.
Laux, Mrs. Samuel C.
*Lawton, Mrs. R. Stanley
Leibman, Mrs. J. H.
Leibrock, Mrs. Edward J.
Lemley, Mrs. Max
Lesher, Mrs. Carl F.
Levin, Mrs. Harold N.
Lichtenauer, Mrs. Robert A.
Lippert, Catherine
Long, Mrs. Clarence
Loomis, Mrs. Robert M.
Lorber, Mrs. Arthur
Louer, Albert O.
Louer, Mrs. Albert O.
Lynch, Mrs. Arthur E.

Mace, Mrs. William M.
*Mackey, Mrs. John
MacNeill, Mrs. Robert S.
Malless, Mrs. Stan
Mantel, Mrs. Thomas D.
Marks, Mrs. Henry M.
Marks, Mrs. Louis
Martin, Miss Isabel K.
Mason, Miss Irene V.
Matthews, Mrs. Walter J.
Maxam, Mrs. B. T.
McClelland, Mrs. Stewart W.
*McDermott, Mrs. James A.
McKown, Mrs. Richard

INDIANAPOLIS COLLECTS & COOKS   201

McMurray, Mrs. T. S., Jr.
Meditch, Mrs. Boris E.
Meek, Mrs. J. Perry
Meshberger, Mrs. Lynn
Miller, Mrs. Blaine, Jr.
Miller, Mrs. Robert A.
Miller, Mrs. Roscoe E.
Minneman, Mrs. John
Mino, Dr. Yutaka
Moberly, Mrs. Warren C.
Monsey, Mrs. Richard E.
Montgomery, Ms. Marianne
Morris, Mrs. Ralph D.
Morton, Mrs. Philip M.
Mosher, Mrs. P. Coon
Mott, Mrs. George M.
Mullin, Mrs. Arthur J.
Murray, Mrs. Marjorie A.
Myers, Mrs. Clarence A.
Myers, Mrs. William M.

Nelson, Mrs. Hugo E.
Neuss, Mrs. Norbert
*Newbold, Mrs. William
Newlund, Mrs. C. E.
Nickel, Ms. Emily
Nie, Mrs. Louis W.

Ohleyer, Mrs. Edward J.
Orr, Mrs. Robert D.
Overman, Mrs. Jesse V.

Palmer, Mrs. Nora
Pantzer, Mrs. John G., Jr.
Parsons, Mrs. Robert W.
Paul, Mrs. Gerald
Payne, Mrs. J. W.
Paynter, Mrs. Morris B.
Payton, Miss Mary M.
*Peacock, Mrs. John E. D.
Pearce, Mrs. Stedman L.
Peck, Mrs. F. Bruce, Jr.
Peters, Mrs. Oscar C.
Petticrew, Mrs. C. R.
Pfleiderer, Mrs. R. J.
Pickering, Mrs. Elizabeth
Pierce, Mrs. Joseph D.
Plaster, Mrs. E. L.
Powell, Mrs. R. R.
Pruyn, Mrs. Theodore M.
Pulliam, Mrs. Eugene S.

Raikos, Mrs. John D.
Ransel, Mrs. J. E.

Reisler, Mrs. Philip
Rhodehamel, Mrs. W. Richard
*Richardson, Mrs. G. E.
Richardson, Mrs. Peter A.
Riggs, Mrs. David A.
Ringgenberg, Mrs. Lyle L.
Ristine, Mrs. Thomas H.
*Ristine, Mrs. Richard O.
Ristine, Mrs. Richard O., Jr.
Ritter, Mrs. FLoyd
Robbins, Mrs. Robert Q.
Roberts, Mrs. Bruce B.
Roberts, Mrs. H. N.
Roberts, Mrs. William E.
Rochford, Mrs. John J.
Rogge, Mrs. James D.
Ruch, Mrs. Stewart E.
Ruebeck, Mrs. Fred W.
Rust, Mrs. Albert M.

St. Angelo, Mrs. Gordon
Schahet, Mrs. Gary A.
Schemmel, Mrs. W. Thomas
Schild, Miss Laura
*Schlegel, Mrs. Fred
Schneider, Mrs. Joseph C.
Schnicke, Mrs. Clarence W.
Schnute, Mrs. Richard B.
Schoberg, Ms. Marjorie R.
Schubert, Mrs. Sy
Schuster, Mrs. Dwight
Scofield, Mrs. John
Seidman, Mrs. Marshall J.
Shawhan, Mrs. Samuel
Shisler, Mrs. Jerry
Shullenberger, Mrs. Gale T.
Shumacker, Mrs. Harris B., Jr.
Simmons, Mrs. Percy
Singleton, Miss Nancy M.
Skole, Mrs. Norman
Smith, Mrs. Wilbur
Snoddy, Mrs. J. Malcolm
Springer, Mrs. Frank C., Jr.
Sputh, Mrs. Fred
Stark, Mrs. George W.
Steele, Mrs. Sydney
Stenacker, Mrs. Jack
Stephens, Mrs. Donald E.
Stiers, Mrs. J. E.
Stoelting, Mrs. V. K.
Stogsdill, Mrs. Willis W.
Stokely, Mrs. Alfred J.
Stokes, Mrs. P. James
Storey, Mrs. V. James

Strader, Mrs. Jack W.
Strain, Mrs. Edward
Strong, Mrs. Charles L.
Supple, Mrs. Graeme B.
Sutherland, Mrs. Donald G.
Sweeney, Mrs. Jerome R.

Todd, Mrs. Thomas E.
*Tolley, Mrs. Michael P.
Tomlinson, Mrs. Willis
Tortorice, Mrs. C. L.
Trefz, Mrs. Alfred A.
Trimpe, Mrs. Earl C.

Vance, Mrs. Carl B.
Vaughn, Mrs. Eugene
Vaught, Mrs. Norbert B.
Vickery, Mrs. George E., Jr.

Wallace, Mrs. F. D., Jr.
Wallace, Robert
Wallace, Mrs. Robert
Wallisa, Mrs. Victor G.
Walsh, Mrs. Matthew P.
*Walton, Mrs. Robert
Ward, Mrs. Irwin A., Jr.
Watson, Mrs. Howard B.
Watts, Mrs. Richard W.
Weber, Mrs. George
Westlund, Mrs. Albert F.
White, Mrs. Arthur C.
White, Mrs. Harold L., Jr.
*White, Mrs. James P.
White, Miss Kathy A.
Wiedemann, Mrs. Frank E.
Wilkerson, Mrs. L. Gale
Wilkins, Mrs. Gene E.
Williams, Mrs. David P., III
Williams, Mrs. R. Marvin
Wolf, Mrs. Fred R.
Wolf, Mrs. Walter E., Jr.
Wood, Mrs. Donald E.
Woodard, Mrs. E. O.
Worth, Mrs. Robert M.
Wurster, Mrs. Fred C.

Yassin, Robert A.
Yassin, Mrs. Robert A.
Young, Mrs. Aribert L.
Young, Mrs. Howard S.

Zimmerman, Mrs. D. G.
Zimmerman, Mrs. W. Paul, Jr.
Zimny, Mrs. Edward B.

INDIANAPOLIS COLLECTS & COOKS
Alliance Publications, Department 200
The Alliance of the Indianapolis Museum of Art
P.O. Box 88236
Indianapolis, Indiana 46208-0236

Please send me _____ copies of INDIANAPOLIS COLLECTS & COOKS.
I am enclosing $11.75 each plus $1.50 each postage and handling.
(Indiana residents add 5% sales tax.)

NAME

ADDRESS

CITY   STATE   ZIP
☐ Check or money order enclosed
Please charge to my ☐ Master Charge   ☐ Visa account

ACC.#   EXPIRES   SIGNATURE

MAIL TO: ALLIANCE PUBLICATIONS, DEPT. 200   All proceeds from the sale of
          P.O. Box 88236   this book are used for the benefit
          Indianapolis, IN 46208-0236   of the Indianapolis Museum of Art.

Please send me _____ copies of INDIANAPOLIS COLLECTS & COOKS.
I am enclosing $11.75 each plus $1.50 each postage and handling.
(Indiana residents add 5% sales tax.)

NAME

ADDRESS

CITY   STATE   ZIP
☐ Check or money order enclosed
Please charge to my ☐ Master Charge   ☐ Visa account

ACC.#   EXPIRES   SIGNATURE

MAIL TO: ALLIANCE PUBLICATIONS, DEPT. 200   All proceeds from the sale of
          P.O. Box 88236   this book are used for the benefit
          Indianapolis, IN 46208-0236   of the Indianapolis Museum of Art.

Please send me _____ copies of INDIANAPOLIS COLLECTS & COOKS.
I am enclosing $11.75 each plus $1.50 each postage and handling.
(Indiana residents add 5% sales tax.)

NAME

ADDRESS

CITY   STATE   ZIP
☐ Check or money order enclosed
Please charge to my ☐ Master Charge   ☐ Visa account

ACC.#   EXPIRES   SIGNATURE

MAIL TO: ALLIANCE PUBLICATIONS, DEPT. 200   All proceeds from the sale of
          P.O. Box 88236   this book are used for the benefit
          Indianapolis, IN 46208-0236   of the Indianapolis Museum of Art.